THE SHIP IN THE DESERT.

THE
SHIP IN THE DESERT.

BY

JOAQUIN MILLER,

AUTHOR OF "SONGS OF THE SIERRAS" AND "SONGS OF THE SUN-LANDS."

BOSTON:
ROBERTS BROTHERS.
1875.

Cambridge:
Press of John Wilson & Son.

DEDICATED

TO

MY DEAR PARENTS,

ON THE FOOTHILLS OF

THE OREGON SIERRAS.

PREFACE.

ITH deep reverence I inscribe these lines, my dear parents, to you. I see you now, away beyond the seas, beyond the lands where the sun goes down in the Pacific like some great ship of fire, resting still on the green hills, watching your herds, waiting

> "Where rolls the Oregon,
> And hears no sound save its own dashing."

Nearly a quarter of a century ago you took me the long and lonesome half-year's journey across the mighty continent, wild, and rent, and broken up, and sown with sand and ashes, and crossed by tumbling, wooded rivers that ran as if glad to get away, fresh and strange and new as if but half-fashioned from the hand of God.

All the time as I tread this strange land I re-live those scenes, and you are with me. How dark and deep, how sullen, strong, and lion-like the mighty Missouri rolled between his walls of untracked wood and cleft the unknown domain of the middle world before us!

Then the frail and buffeted rafts on the river, the women and children huddled together, the shouts of the brawny men as they swam with the bellowing cattle; the cows in the stormy stream, eddying, whirling, spinning about, calling to their young, their bright horns shining in the sun. . . . The wild men waiting on the other side, painted savages leaning silent on their bows, despising our weakness, opening a way, letting us pass on to the unknown distances, where they said the sun and moon lay down together and brought forth the stars. . . . The long and winding lines of wagons, the graves by the wayside, the women weeping together as they passed on. Then hills, then plains, parched lands like Syria, dust, and ashes, and alkali, cool streams with woods, camps by night, great wood fires in circles, tents in the centre like Cæsar's battle-camps, painted men that passed like shadows, showers of arrows, the wild beasts howling from the hill. . . .

You, my dear parents, will pardon the thread of fiction on which I have strung these scenes and descriptions of a mighty land of mystery, and wild and savage grandeur, for the world will have its way, and, like a spoiled child, demands a tale.

> "Yea,
> We who toil and earn our bread
> Still have our masters. . . ."

A ragged and broken story it is, with long deserts, with alkali and ashes, yet it may, like the land it deals of, have some green places, and woods, and running waters, where you can rest. . . .

Three times now I have ranged the great West in fancy, as I did in fact for twenty years, and gathered unknown and unnamed blossoms from mountain-top, from desert level, where man never ranged before, and asked the world to receive my weeds, my grasses, and blue-eyed blossoms. But here it ends. Good or bad, I have done enough of this work on the border. The Orient promises a more grateful harvest.

I have been true to my West. She has been my only love. I have remembered her greatness. I have done my work to show to the world her vastness, her riches, her resources, her valor and her dignity, her poetry and her grandeur. Yet while I was going on, working so in silence, what were the things she said of me? But let that pass, my dear parents. Others will come after us. Possibly I have blazed out the trail for great minds over this field, as you did across the deserts and plains for great men a quarter of a century ago.

JOAQUIN MILLER.

Lake Como, Italy.

THE SHIP IN THE DESERT.

I.

MAN in middle Aridzone
Stood by the desert's edge alone,
And long he look'd, and lean'd.
He peer'd,
Above his twirl'd and twisted beard,
Beneath his black and slouchy hat . . .
Nay, nay, the tale is not of that.

A skin-clad trapper, toe-a-tip,
Stood on a mountain top, and he
Look'd long and still and eagerly.
"It looks so like some lonesome ship

That sails this ghostly lonely sea,—
This dried-up desert sea," said he,
"These tawny sands of Arazit" . . .
Avaunt! the tale is not of it.

A chief from out the desert's rim
Rode swift as twilight swallows swim,
Or eagle blown from eyrie nest.
His trim-limb'd steed was black as night,
His long black hair had blossom'd white,
With feathers from the koko's crest;
His iron face was flush'd and red,
His eyes flash'd fire as he fled,
For he had seen unsightly things;
Had felt the flapping of their wings.

A wild and wiry man was he,
This tawny chief of Shoshonee;
And O his supple steed was fleet!
About his breast flapp'd panther skins,

About his eager flying feet
Flapp'd beaded, braided moccasins:
He rode as rides the hurricane;
He seem'd to swallow up the plain;
He rode as never man did ride,
He rode, for ghosts rode at his side,
And on his right a grizzled grim —
No, no, this tale is not of him.

An Indian warrior lost his way
While prowling on this desert's edge
In fragrant sage and prickly hedge,
When suddenly he saw a sight,
And turn'd his steed in eager flight.
He rode right through the edge of day,
He rode into the rolling night.

He lean'd, he reach'd an eager face,
His black wolf skin flapp'd out and in,
And tiger claws on tiger skin

Held seat and saddle to its place;
But that gray ghost that clutch'd thereat . . .
Arrête! the tale is not of that.

A chieftain touch'd the desert's rim
One autumn eve: he rode alone
And still as moon-made shadows swim.
He stopp'd, he stood as still as stone,
He lean'd, he look'd, there glisten'd bright
From out the yellow yielding sand
A golden cup with jewell'd rim.
He lean'd him low, he reach'd a hand,
He caught it up, he gallop'd on,
He turn'd his head, he saw a sight . . .
His panther skins flew to the wind,
The dark, the desert lay behind;
The tawny Ishmaelite was gone;
But something sombre as death is . . .
Tut, tut! the tale is not of this.

A mountaineer, storm-stained and brown,
From farthest desert touched the town,
And, striding through the crowd, held up
Above his head a jewell'd cup.
He put two fingers to his lip,
He whisper'd wild, he stood a-tip,
And lean'd the while with lifted hand,
And said, "A ship lies yonder dead,"
And said, "Doubloons lie sown in sand
In yon far desert dead and brown,
Beyond where wave-wash'd walls look down,
As thick as stars set overhead.
That three shipmasts uplift like trees" . . .
Away! the tale is not of these.

An Indian hunter held a plate
Of gold above his lifted head,
Around which kings had sat in state . . .
"'Tis from that desert ship," they said,
"That sails with neither sail nor breeze,

Or galleon, that sank below
Of old, in olden dried-up seas,
Ere yet the red men drew the bow."

But wrinkled women wagg'd the head,
And walls of warriors sat that night
In black, nor streak of battle red,
Around against the red camp light,
And told such wondrous tales as these
Of wealth within their dried-up seas.

And one, girt well in tiger's skin,
Who stood, like Saul, above the rest,
With dangling claws about his breast,
A belt without, a blade within,
A warrior with a painted face,
And lines that shadow'd stern and grim,
Stood pointing east from his high place,
And hurling thought like cannon shot,
Stood high with visage flush'd and hot . . .
But, stay! this tale is not of him.

II.

By Arizona's sea of sand
Some bearded miners, gray and old,
And resolute in search of gold,
Sat down to tap the savage land.

They tented in a cañon's mouth
That gaped against the warm wide south,
And underneath a wave-wash'd wall,
Where now nor rains nor winds may fall,
They delved the level salt-white sands
For gold, with bold and hornéd hands.

A miner stood beside his mine,
He pull'd his beard, then look'd away
Across the level sea of sand,
Beneath his broad and hairy hand,
A hand as hard as knots of pine.

" It looks so like a sea," said he.
He pull'd his beard, and he did say,
" It looks just like a dried-up sea."
Again he pull'd that beard of his,
But said no other thing than this.

A stalwart miner dealt a stroke,
And struck a buried beam of oak.
An old ship's beam the shaft appear'd,
With storm-worn faded figure-head.
The miner twisted, twirled his beard,
Lean'd on his pick-axe as he spoke:
" 'Tis from some long-lost ship," he said,
" Some laden ship of Solomon
That sail'd these lonesome seas upon
In search of Ophir's mine, ah me!
That sail'd this dried-up desert sea." . . .
Nay, nay, 'tis not a tale of gold,
But ghostly land storm-slain and old.

III.

But this the tale. Along a wide
And sounding stream some silent braves,
That stole along the farther side
Through sweeping wood that swept the waves
Like long arms reach'd across the tide,
Kept watch and ward and still defied. . . .

A low black boat that hugg'd the shores,
An ugly boat, an ugly crew,
Thick-lipp'd and woolly-headed slaves,
That bow'd, that bent the white-ash oars,
That cleft the murky waters through,
That climb'd the swift Missouri's waves,—
The surly, woolly-headed slaves.

A grand old Neptune in the prow,
Gray-hair'd, and white with touch of time,

Yet strong as in his middle prime;
A grizzled king, I see him now,
With beard as blown by wind of seas,
And wild and white as white sea-storm,
Stand up, turn suddenly, look back
Along the low boat's wrinkled track,
Then fold his mantle round a form
Broad-built as any Hercules,
And so sit silently.

Beside
The grim old sea-king sits his bride,
A sun-land blossom, rudely torn
From tropic forests to be worn
Above as stern a breast as e'er
Stood king at sea or anywhere. . . .

Another boat with other crew
Came swift and silent in her track,
And now shot shoreward, now shot back,
And now sat rocking fro and to,

But never once lost sight of her.
Tall, sunburnt, southern men were these
From isles of blue Caribbean seas,
And one, that woman's worshipper,
Who looked on her, and loved but her.

And one, that one, was wild as seas
That wash the far dark Oregon,
And ever leaning, urging on,
And standing up in restless ease,
He seem'd as lithe and free and tall
And restless as the boughs that stir
Perpetual topt poplar trees.
And one, that one, had eyes to teach
The art of love, and tongue to preach
Life's hard and sober homilies;
And yet his eager hands, his speech,
All spoke the bold adventurer;
While zoned about the belt of each
There swung a girt of steel, till all
Did seem a walking arsenal.

IV.

PURSUER and pursued. And who
Are these that make the sable crew ;
These mighty Titans, black and nude,
And hairy-breasted, bronzed and broad
Of chest as any demi-god,
That dare this peopled solitude ?

And who is he that leads them here,
And breaks the hush of wave and wood ?
Comes he for evil or for good ?
Brave Jesuit or bold buccaneer ?

Nay, these be idle themes. Let pass.
These be but men. We may forget
The wild sea-king, the tawny brave,
The frowning wold, the woody shore,
The tall-built, sunburnt men of Mars. . . .

But what and who was she, the fair?
The fairest face that ever yet
Look'd in a wave as in a glass;
That look'd as look the still, far stars,
So woman-like, into the wave
To contemplate their beauty there,
Yet look as looking anywhere?

And who of all the world was she?
A bride, or not a bride? A thing
To love? A prison'd bird to sing?
You shall not know. That shall not be
Brought from the future's great profound
This side the happy hunting-ground.

I only saw her, heard the sound
Of murky waters gurgling round
In counter-currents from the shore,
But heard the long, strong stroke of oar
Against the waters gray and vast.
I only saw her as she pass'd —

A great, sad beauty, in whose eyes
Lay all the loves of Paradise. . . .

You shall not know her — she who sat
Unconscious in my heart all time
I dream'd and wove this wayward rhyme,
And loved and did not blush thereat.

The sunlight of a sunlit land,
A land of fruit, of flowers, and
A land of love and calm delight ;
A land where night is not like night,
And noon is but a name for rest,
And love for love is reckoned best.

Where conversations of the eyes
Are all enough ; where beauty thrills
The heart like hues of harvest-home ;
Where rage lies down, where passion dies,
Where peace hath her abiding place. . . .

A face that lifted up; sweet face
That was so like a life begun,
That rose for me a rising sun
Above the bended seven hills
Of dead and risen old new Rome.

Not that I deem'd she loved me. Nay,
I dared not even dream of that.
I only say I knew her; say
She ever sat before me, sat
All still and voiceless as love is,
And ever look'd so fair, divine,
Her hush'd, vehement soul fill'd mine,
And overflowed with Runic bliss,
And made itself a part of this.

O you had loved her sitting there,
Half hidden in her loosen'd hair:
Why, you had loved her for her eyes,
Their large and melancholy look

Of tenderness, and well mistook
Their love for light of Paradise.

Yea, loved her for her large dark eyes ;
Yea, loved her for her brow's soft brown ;
Her hand as light as heaven's bars ;
Yea, loved her for her mouth. Her mouth
Was roses gather'd from the south,
The warm south side of Paradise,
And breathed upon and handed down,
By angels on a stair of stars.

Her mouth ! 'twas Egypt's mouth of old,
Push'd out and pouting full and bold
With simple beauty where she sat.
Why, you had said, on seeing her,
This creature comes from out the dim
Far centuries, beyond the rim
Of time's remotest reach or stir.
And he who wrought Semiramis

And shaped the Sibyls, seeing this,
Had bow'd and made a shrine thereat,
And all his life had worshipp'd her,
Devout as north-Nile worshipper.

I dared not dream she loved me. Nay,
Her love was proud ; and pride is loth
To look with favor, own it fond
Of one the world loves not to-day. . . .
No matter if she loved or no,
God knows I loved enough for both,
And knew her as you shall not know
Till you have known sweet death, and you
Have cross'd the dark ; gone over to
The great majority beyond.

V.

THE black men bow'd, the long oars bent,
They struck as if for sweet life's sake,
And one look'd back, but no man spake,
And all wills bent to one intent.

On through the golden fringe of day
Into the deep, dark night, away
And up the wave 'mid walls of wood
They cleft, they climb'd, they bowed, they
    bent,
But one stood tall, and restless stood,
And one sat still all night, all day,
And gazed in helpless wonderment.

Her hair pour'd down like darkling wine,
The black men lean'd, a sullen line,

The bent oars kept a steady song,
And all the beams of bright sunshine
That touch'd the waters wild and strong,
Fell drifting down and out of sight
Like fallen leaves, and it was night.

And night and day, and many days
They climb'd the sudden, dark gray tide,
And she sat silent at his side,
And he sat turning many ways:

Sat watching for his wily foe;
At last he baffled him. And yet
His brow gloom'd dark, his lips were set;
He lean'd, he peer'd through boughs, as though
From heart of forests deep and dim
Grim shapes could come confronting him.

A grand, uncommon man was he,
Broad-shoulder'd, and of Gothic form,

Strong-built, and hoary like a sea;
A high sea broken up by storm.

His face was brown and overwrought
By seams and shadows born of thought,
Not over gentle. And his eyes,
Bold, restless, resolute, and deep,
Too deep to flow like shallow fount
Of common men where waters mount
And men bend down their heads and weep —
Fierce, lumin'd eyes, where flames might rise
Instead of flood, and flash and sweep —
Strange eyes, that look'd unsatisfied
With all things fair or otherwise;
As if his inmost soul had cried
All time for something yet unseen,
Some long-desired thing denied.

A man whose soul was mightier far
Than his great self, and surged and fell

About himself as heaving seas
Lift up and lash, and boom, and swell
Above some solitary bar
That bursts through blown Samoa's sea,
And wreck and toss eternally.

VI.

BELOW the overhanging boughs
The oars laid idle at the last.
Yet long he look'd for hostile prows
From out the wood and down the stream.
They came not, and he came to dream
Pursuit abandon'd, danger past.

He fell'd the oak, he built a home
Of new-hewn wood with busy hand,
And said, "My wanderings are told."
And said, "No more by sea, by land,
Shall I break rest, or drift, or roam,
For I am worn, and I grow old."

And there, beside that surging tide,
Where gray waves meet, and wheel, and strike,
The man sat down as satisfied

To sit and rest unto the end;
As if the strong man here had found
A sort of brother in this sea, —
This surging, sounding majesty
Of troubled water, so profound,
So sullen, strong, and lion-like,
So sinuous and foamy bound.

Hast seen Missouri cleave the wood
In sounding whirlpools to the sea?
What soul hath known such majesty?
What man stood by and understood?

By pleasant Omaha I stood,
Beneath a fringe of mailèd wood,
And watch'd the mighty waters heave,
And surge, and strike, and wind, and weave,
And make strange sounds and mutterings,
As if of dark unutter'd things.

By pleasant high-built Omaha
I stand. The waves beneath me run
All stain'd and yellow, dark and dun,
And deep as death's sweet mystery, —
A thousand Tibers roll'd in one.
I count on other years. I draw
The curtain from the scenes to be.
I see another Rome. I see
A Cæsar tower in the land,
And take her in his iron hand.
I see a throne, a king, a crown,
A high-built capital thrown down.

I see my river rise . . .
Away!
The world's cold commerce of to-day
Demands some idle flippant theme;
And I, your minstrel, must sit by,
And harp along the edge of morn,
And sing and celebrate to please

The multitude, the mob, and these
They know not pearls from yellow corn.
Yea, idly sing or silent dream ;
My harp, my hand is yours, but I —
My soul moves down that sounding stream.

Adieu, dun, mighty stream, adieu!
Adown thine wooded walls, inwrought
With rose of Cherokee and vine,
Was never heard a minstrel's note,
And none would heed a song of mine.
I find expression for my thought
In other themes. . . . List! I have seen
A grizzly sporting on the green
Of west sierras with a goat,
And finding pastime all day through. . . .

O sounding, swift Missouri, born
Of Rocky Mountains, and begot
On bed of snow at birth of morn,

Of thunder-storms and elements
That reign where puny man comes not,
With fountain-head in fields of gold,
And wide arms twining wood and wold,
And everlasting snowy tents, —
I hail you from the Orients.

Shall I return to you once more?
Shall take occasion by the throat
And thrill with wild Æolian note?
Shall sit and sing by your deep shore?
Shall shape a reed and pipe of yore
And wake old melodies made new,
And thrill thine leaf-land through and through?

VII.

THEN long the long oars idle lay.
The cabin's smoke came forth and curl'd
Right lazily from river brake,
And Time went by the other way.
And who was she, the strong man's pride?
This one fair woman of the world.
A captive? Bride, or not a bride?
Her eyes, men say, grew sad and dim
With watching from the river's rim,
As waiting for some face denied.
And yet she never wept or spake,
Or breath'd his name for her love's sake.

Yea, who was she? — none ever knew.
The great strong river swept around,
The cabins nestled in its bend,
But kept its secrets. Wild birds flew

In bevies by. The black men found
Diversion in the chase: and wide
Old Morgan ranged the wood, nor friend,
Nor foeman ever at his side
Or shared his forests deep and dim,
Or cross'd his path or question'd him.

He stood as one who found and named
The middle world. What visions flamed
Athwart the west! What prophecies
Were his, the gray old man, that day
Who stood alone and look'd away, —
Awest from out the waving trees,
Against the utter sundown seas.

Alone oft-time beside the stream
He stood and gazed as in a dream,
As if he knew a life unknown
To those who knew him thus alone.

His eyes were gray and overborne

By shaggy brows, his strength was shorn,
Yet still he ever gazed awest,
As one who would not, could not rest.

And whence came he? and when, and why?
Men question'd men, but nought was known
Save that he roam'd the woods alone,
And lived alone beneath the stir
Of leaves, and letting life go by,
Did look on her and only her.

And had he fled with bloody hand?
Or had he loved some Helen fair,
And battling lost both land and town?
Say, did he see his walls go down,
Then choose from all his treasures there
This love, and seek some other land?

And yet the current of his life
Mostlike had flow'd like oil; had been

A monk's, for aught that all men knew.
Mostlike the sad man's only sin,
A cruel one, for thought is strife,
Had been the curse of thought all through.

Mayhap his splendid soul had spurn'd
Insipid, sweet society,
That stinks in nostrils of all men
High-born and fearless-souled and free;—
That tasting to satiety
Her hollow sweets he proudly turn'd,
And did rebel and curse her then;
And then did stoop and from the sod
Pluck this one flower for his breast,
Then turn to solitude for rest,
And turn from man in search of God.

And as to that, I reckon it
But right, but Christian-like and just,
And closer after Christ's own plan,

To take men as you find your man,
To take a soul from God on trust,
A fit man, or yourself unfit:

To take man free from the control
Of man's opinion: take a soul
In its own troubled world, all fair
As you behold it then and there,
Set naked in your sight, alone,
Unnamed, unheralded, unknown:

Yea, take him bravely from the hand
That reach'd him forth from nothingness,
That took his tired soul to keep
All night, then reach'd him out from sleep
And sat him equal in the land;
Sent out from where the angels are,
A soul new-born, without one whit
Of bought or borrow'd character.

Ah, bless us! if we only could

As ready spin and willing weave
Sweet tales of charity and good ;
Could we as willing clip the wings
Of cruel tales as pleasant things,
How sweet 'twould then be to believe,
How good 'twould then be to be good.

VIII.

THE squirrels chatter'd in the leaves,
The turkeys call'd from pawpaw wood,
The deer with lifted nostrils stood,
And humming-birds did wind and weave,
Swim round about, dart in and out,
Through fragrant forest edge made red,
Made many-colour'd overhead
By climbing blossoms sweet with bee
And yellow rose of Cherokee.

Then frosts came by and touch'd the leaves,
Then time hung ices on the eaves,
Then cushion snows possess'd the ground,
And so the seasons kept their round;
Yet still old Morgan went and came
From cabin door to forest dim,
Through wold of snows, through wood of flame,

Through golden Indian-summer days,
Hung round in soft September haze,
And no man cross'd or question'd him.

Nay, there was that in his stern air
That held e'en these rude men aloof:
None came to share the broad-built roof
That rose so fortress-like beside
The angry, rushing, sullen tide,
And only black men gather'd there,
The old man's slaves, in dull content,
Black, silent, and obedient.

Then men push'd westward through his wood,
His wild beasts fled, and now he stood
Confronting men. He had endear'd
No man, but still he went and came
Apart, and shook his beard and strode
His ways alone, and bore his load,
If load it were, apart, alone.

Then men grew busy with a name
That no man loved, that many fear'd,
And cowards stoop'd, and cast a stone,
As at some statue overthrown.

Some said a pirate blown by night
From isles of calm Caribbean land,
Who left his comrades ; that he fled
With many prices on his head,
And that he bore in his hot flight
The gather'd treasure of his band,
In bloody and unholy hand.

Then some did say a privateer,
Then others, that he fled from fear,
And climb'd the mad Missouri far,
To where the friendly forests are ;
And that his illy-gotten gold
Lay sunken in his black boat's hold.
Then others, watching his fair bride,
Said, " There is something more beside."

Some said, a stolen bride was she,
And that his strong arm in the strife
Was red with her own brother's life,
And that her lover from the sea
Lay waiting for his chosen wife,
And that a day of reckoning
Lay waiting for this grizzled king.

O sweet child-face, that ever gazed
From out the wood and down the wave!
O eyes, that never once were raised!
O mouth, that never murmur gave!

IX.

O DARK-EYED Ina! All the years
Brought her but solitude and tears.
Lo! ever looking out she stood
Adown the wave, adown the wood,
Adown the strong stream to the south,
Sad-faced, and sorrowful. Her mouth
Push'd out so pitiful. Her eyes
Fill'd full of sorrow and surprise.

Men say that looking from her place
A love would sometimes light her face,
As if sweet recollections stirr'd
Her heart and broke its loneliness,
Like far sweet songs that come to us,
So soft, so sweet, they are not heard,

So far, so faint, they fill the air,
A fragrance filling anywhere.

And wasting all her summer years
That utter'd only through her tears,
The seasons went, and still she stood
For ever watching down the wood.

Yet in her heart there held a strife
With all this wasting of sweet life
That none who have not lived and died,
Held up the two hands crucified
Between the ways on either hand,
Can look upon or understand.

The blackest rain-clouds muffle fire:
Between a duty and desire
There lies no middle way or land:
Take thou the right or the left hand,
And so pursue, nor hesitate
To boldly give your hand to fate.

In helpless indecisions lie
The rocks on which we strike and die.
'Twere better far to choose the worst
Of all life's ways than to be cursed
With indecision. Turn and choose
Your way, then all the world refuse.

And men who saw her still do say
That never once her lips were heard,
By gloaming dusk or shining day,
To utter or pronounce one word.
Men went and came, and still she stood
In silence watching down the wood.

Yea, still she stood and look'd away,
By tawny night, by fair-fac'd day,
Adown the wood beyond the land,
Her hollow face upon her hand,
Her black, abundant hair all down
About her loose, ungather'd gown.

And what her thought? her life unsaid?
Was it of love? of hate? of him,
The tall, dark Southerner?
Her head
Bow'd down. The day fell dim
Upon her eyes. She bow'd, she slept.
She waken'd then, and waking wept.

She dream'd, perchance, of island home,
A land of palms ring'd round with foam,
Where summer on her shelly shore
Sits down and rests for evermore.

And one who watch'd her wasted youth
Did guess, mayhap with much of truth,
Her heart was with that band that came
Against her isle with sword and flame:
And this the tale he told of her
And her fierce, silent follower:

A Spaniard and adventurer,
A man who saw her, loved, and fell
Upon his knees and worshipp'd her;
And with that fervor and mad zeal
That only sunborn bosoms feel,
Did vow to love, to follow her
Unto the altar . . . or to hell:

That then her gray-hair'd father bore
The beauteous maiden hurriedly
From out her fair isle of the sea
To sombre wold and woody shore
And far away, and kept her well,
As from a habitant of hell,
And vow'd she should not meet him more:
That fearing still the buccaneer,
He silent kept his forests here.
The while men came, and still she stood
For ever watching from the wood.

X.

The black-eyed bushy squirrels ran
Like shadows shatter'd through the boughs;
The gallant robin chirp'd his vows,
The far-off pheasant thrumm'd his fan,
A thousand blackbirds were a-wing
In walnut-top, and it was spring.

Old Morgan left his cabin door,
And one sat watching as of yore;
But why turned Morgan's face as white
As his white beard?
A bird aflight,
A squirrel peering through the trees,
Saw some one silent steal away
Like darkness from the face of day,
Saw two black eyes look back, and these
Saw her hand beckon through the trees.

He knew him, though he had not seen
That form or face for a decade,
Though time had shorn his locks, had made
His form another's, flow'd between
Their lives like some uncompass'd sea,
Yet still he knew him as before.
He pursed his lips, and silently
He turn'd and sought his cabin's door.

Ay! they have come, the sun-brown'd men,
To beard old Morgan in his den.
It matters little who they are,
These silent men from isles afar,
And truly no one cares or knows
What be their merit or demand;
It is enough for this rude land—
At least, it is enough for those,
The loud of tongue and rude of hand—
To know that they are Morgan's foes.

Proud Morgan! More than tongue can tell
He loved that woman watching there,
That stood in her dark stream of hair,
That stood and dream'd as in a spell,
And look'd so fix'd and far away.
And who, that loveth woman well,
Is wholly bad? be who he may.

Ay! we have seen these Southern men,
These sun-brown'd men from island shore,
In this same land, and long before.
They do not seem so lithe as then,
They do not look so tall, and they
Seem not so many as of old.
But that same resolute and bold
Expression of unbridled will,
That even Time must half obey,
Is with them and is of them still.

They do not counsel the decree
Of court or council, where they drew

Their breath, nor law nor order knew,
Save but the strong hand of the strong;
Where each stood up, avenged his wrong,
Or sought his death all silently.

They watch along the wave and wood,
They heed, but haste not. Their estate,
Whate'er it be, can bide and wait,
Be it open ill or hidden good.

No law for them! For they have stood
With steel, and writ their rights in blood;
And now, whatever 'tis they seek,
Whatever be their dark demand,
Why, they will make it, hand to hand,
Take time and patience: Greek to Greek.

XI.

LIKE blown and snowy wintry pine,
Old Morgan stoop'd his head and pass'd
Within his cabin door. He cast
A great arm out to men, made sign,
Then turned to Ina; stood beside
A time, then turn'd and strode the floor,
Stopp'd short, breathed sharp, threw wide the door,
Then gazed beyond the murky tide,
Toward where the forky peaks divide.

He took his beard in his hard hand,
Then slowly shook his grizzled head
And trembled, but no word he said.
His thought was something more than pain;
Upon the seas, upon the land
He knew he should not rest again.

He turn'd to her ; but then once more
Quick turn'd, and through the oaken door
He sudden pointed to the west.
His eye resumed its old command,
The conversation of his hand,
It was enough : she knew the rest.

He turn'd, he stoop'd, and smoothed her
hair,
As if to smooth away the care
From his great heart, with his left hand.
His right hand hitch'd the pistol round
That dangled at his belt . . .
The sound
Of steel to him was melody
More sweet than any song of sea.

He touch'd his pistol, press'd his lips,
Then tapp'd it with his finger-tips,
And toy'd with it as harper's hand

Seeks out the chords when he is sad
And purposeless.
At last he had
Resolved. In haste he touch'd her hair,
Made sign she should arise — prepare
For some long journey, then again
He look'd awest toward the plain:

Toward the land of dreams and space,
The land of Silences, the land
Of shoreless deserts sown with sand,
Where desolation's dwelling is:
The land where, wondering, you say,
What dried-up shoreless sea is this?
Where, wandering, from day to day
You say, To-morrow sure we come
To rest in some cool resting-place,
And yet you journey on through space
While seasons pass, and are struck dumb
With marvel at the distances.

Yea, he would go. Go utterly
Away, and from all living kind,
Pierce through the distances, and find
New lands. He had outlived his race.
He stood like some eternal tree
That tops remote Yosemite,
And cannot fall. He turn'd his face
Again and contemplated space.

And then he raised his hand to vex
His beard, stood still, and there fell down
Great drops from some unfrequent spring,
And streak'd his channell'd cheeks sun-
brown,
And ran uncheck'd, as one who recks
Nor joy, nor tears, nor any thing.

And then, his broad breast heaving deep,
Like some dark sea in troubled sleep,
Blown round with groaning ships and wrecks,

He sudden roused himself, and stood
With all the strength of his stern mood,
Then call'd his men, and bade them go
And bring black steeds with banner'd necks,
And strong like burly buffalo.

XII.

THE sassafras took leaf, and men
Push'd west in hosts. The black men drew
Their black-maned horses silent through
The solemn woods.
One midnight when
The curl'd moon tipp'd her horn, and threw
A black oak's shadow slant across
A low mound hid in leaves and moss,
Old Morgan cautious came and drew
From out the ground, as from a grave,
A great box, iron-bound and old,
And fill'd, men say, with pirates' gold,
And then they, silent as a dream,
In long black shadows cross'd the stream.

Lo! here the smoke of cabins curl'd,
The borders of the middle world;

And mighty, hairy, half-wild men
Sat down in silence, held at bay
By mailèd forests. Far away
The red men's boundless borders lay,
And lodges stood in legions then,
Strip'd pyramids of painted men

What strong uncommon men were these,
These settlers hewing to the seas!
Great horny-handed men and tan;
Men blown from any border land;
Men desperate and red of hand,
And men in love and men in debt,
And men who lived but to forget,
And men whose very hearts had died,
Who only sought these woods to hide
Their wretchedness, held in the van;
Yet every man among them stood
Alone, along that sounding wood,
And every man somehow a man.

A race of unnamed giants these,
That moved like gods among the trees,
So stern, so stubborn-brow'd and slow,
With strength of black-maned buffalo,
And each man notable and tall,
A kingly and unconscious Saul,
A sort of sullen Hercules.

A star stood large and white awest,
Then Time uprose and testified;
They push'd the mailèd wood aside,
They toss'd the forest like a toy,
That great forgotten race of men,
The boldest band that yet has been
Together since the siege of Troy,
And followed it . . . . and found their rest.

What strength! what strife! what rude
unrest!
What shocks! what half-shaped armies met!

A mighty nation moving west,
With all its steely sinews set
Against the living forests. Hear
The shouts, the shots of pioneer!
The rended forests, rolling wheels,
As if some half-check'd army reels,
Recoils, redoubles, comes again,
Loud sounding like a hurricane.

O bearded, stalwart, westmost men,
So tower-like, so Gothic-built!
A kingdom won without the guilt
Of studied battle; that hath been
Your blood's inheritance . . . .
Your heirs
Know not your tombs. The great ploughshares
Cleave softly through the mellow loam
Where you have made eternal home
And set no sign.
Your epitaphs

Are writ in furrows. Beauty laughs
While through the green ways wandering
Beside her love, slow gathering
White starry-hearted May-time blooms
Above your lowly levell'd tombs ;
And then below the spotted sky
She stops, she leans, she wonders why
The ground is heaved and broken so,
And why the grasses darker grow
And droop and trail like wounded wing.

Yea, Time, the grand old harvester,
Has gather'd you from wood and plain.
We call to you again, again ;
The rush and rumble of the car
Comes back in answer. Deep and wide
The wheels of progress have pass'd on ;
The silent pioneer is gone.
His ghost is moving down the trees,
And now we push the memories

Of bluff, bold men who dared and died
In foremost battle, quite aside.

O perfect Eden of the earth,
In poppies sown, in harvest set!
O sires, mothers of my West!
How shall we count your proud bequest?
But yesterday ye gave us birth;
We eat your hard-earn'd bread to-day,
Nor toil nor spin nor make regret,
But praise our petty selves and say
How great we are, and all forget
The still endurance of the rude
Unpolish'd sons of solitude.

XIII.

And one was glad at morn, but one,
The tall old sea-king, grim and gray,
Look'd back to where his cabins lay
And seem'd to hesitate.
He rose
At last, as from his dream's repose,
From rest that counterfeited rest,
And set his blown beard to the west,
And drove against the setting sun,
Along the levels vast and dun.

His steeds were steady, strong, and fleet,
The best in all the wide west land,
Their manes were in the air, their feet
Seem'd scarce to touch the flying sand;
The reins were in the reaching hand.

They rode like men gone mad, they fled,
All day and many days they ran,
And in the rear a gray old man
Kept watch, and ever turn'd his head,
Half eager and half angry, back
Along their dusty desert track.

And one look'd back, but no man spoke,
They rode, they swallow'd up the plain;
The sun sank low, he look'd again,
With lifted hand and shaded eyes.
Then far arear he saw uprise,
As if from giant's stride or stroke,
Dun dust-like puffs of battle-smoke.

He turn'd, his left hand clutch'd the rein,
He struck awest his high right hand,
His arms were like the limbs of oak,
They knew too well the man's command,
They mounted, plunged ahead again,

And one look'd back, but no man spoke,
Of all that sullen iron band,
That reached along that barren land.

O weary days of weary blue,
Without one changing breath, without
One single cloud-ship sailing through
The blue seas bending round about
In one unbroken blotless hue.
Yet on they fled, and one look'd back
For ever down their distant track.

The tent is pitch'd, the blanket spread,
The earth receives the weary head,
The night rolls west, the east is gray,
The tent is struck, they mount, away;
They ride for life the livelong day,
They sweep the long grass in their track,
And one leads on, and one looks back.

What scenes they pass'd, what camps at
morn,
What weary columns kept the road;
What herds of troubled cattle low'd,
And trumpeted like lifted horn;
And everywhere, or road or rest,
All things were pointing to the west;
A weary, long, and lonesome track,
And all led on, but one look'd back.

They climb'd the rock-built breasts of earth,
The Titan-fronted, blowy steeps
That cradled Time . . . Where Freedom keeps
Her flag of white blown stars unfurl'd,
They turn'd about, they saw the birth
Of sudden dawn upon the world;
Again they gazed; they saw the face
Of God, and named it boundless space.

And they descended and did roam

Through levell'd distances set round
By room. They saw the Silences
Move by and beckon : saw the forms,
The very beards, of burly storms,
And heard them talk like sounding seas.
On unnamed heights bleak-blown and brown,
And torn like battlements of Mars,
They saw the darknesses come down,
Like curtains loosen'd from the dome
Of God's cathedral, built of stars.

They pitch'd the tent, where rivers run
As if to drown the falling sun.
They saw the snowy mountains roll'd,
And heaved along the nameless lands
Like mighty billows ; saw the gold
Of awful sunsets ; saw the blush
Of sudden dawn, and felt the hush
Of heaven when the day sat down,
And hid his face in dusky hands.

The long and lonesome nights ! the tent
That nestled soft in sweep of grass,
The hills against the firmament
Where scarce the moving moon could pass ;
The cautious camp, the smother'd light,
The silent sentinel at night !

The wild beasts howling from the hill ;
The troubled cattle bellowing ;
The savage prowling by the spring,
Then sudden passing swift and still,
And bended as a bow is bent.
The arrow sent ; the arrow spent
And buried in its bloody place,
The dead man lying on his face !

The clouds of dust, their cloud by day ;
Their pillar of unfailing fire
The far North star. And high, and
higher . . .

They climb'd so high it seem'd eftsoon
That they must face the falling moon,
That like some flame-lit ruin lay
Thrown down before their weary way.

They learn'd to read the sign of storms,
The moon's wide circles, sunset bars,
And storm-provoking blood and flame;
And, like the Chaldean shepherds, came
At night to name the moving stars.
In heaven's face they pictured forms
Of beasts, of fishes of the sea.
They mark'd the Great Bear wearily
Rise up and drag his clinking chain
Of stars around the starry main.

What lines of yoked and patient steers!
What weary thousands pushing west!
What restless pilgrims seeking rest,
As if from out the edge of years!

What great yoked brutes with briskets low,
With wrinkled necks like buffalo,
With round, brown, liquid, pleading eyes,
That turn'd so slow and sad to you,
That shone like love's eyes soft with tears,
That seem'd to plead, and make replies
The while they bow'd their necks and drew
The creaking load; and look'd at you.
Their sable briskets swept the ground,
Their cloven feet kept solemn sound.

Two sullen bullocks led the line,
Their great eyes shining bright like wine;
Two sullen captive kings were they,
That had in time held herds at bay,
And even now they crush'd the sod
With stolid sense of majesty,
And stately stepp'd and stately trod,
As if 'twas something still to be
Kings even in captivity.

XIV.

AND why did these same sunburnt men
Let Morgan gain the plain, and then
Pursue him to the utter sea?
You ask me here impatiently.
And I as pertly must reply,
My task is but to tell a tale,
To give a wide sail to the gale,
To paint the boundless plain, the sky;
To rhyme, nor give a reason why.

Mostlike they sought his gold alone,
And fear'd to make their quarrel known
Lest it should keep its secret bed;
Mostlike they thought to best prevail
And conquer with united hands
Alone upon the lonesome sands;
Mostlike they had as much to dread;
Mostlike — but I must tell my tale.

And Morgan, ever looking back,
Push'd on, push'd up his mountain track,
Past camp, past train, past caravan,
Past flying beast, past failing man,
Past brave men battling with a foe
That circled them with lance and bow
And feather'd arrows all a-wing;
Till months unmeasured came and ran
The calendar with him, as though
Old Time had lost all reckoning;
Then passed for aye the creaking trains,
And pioneers that named the plains.

Those brave old bricks of Forty-nine!
What lives they lived! what deaths they
died!
A thousand cañons, darkling wide
Below Sierra's slopes of pine,
Receive them now.
And they who died

Along the far, dim, desert route.
Their ghosts are many.
Let them keep
Their vast possessions.
The Piute,
The tawny warrior, will dispute
No boundary with these. And I,
Who saw them live, who felt them die,
Say, let their unploughed ashes sleep,
Untouched by man, by plain or steep.

The bearded, sunbrown'd men who bore
The burthen of that frightful year,
Who toil'd, but did not gather store,
They shall not be forgotten.
Drear
And white, the plains of Shoshonee
Shall point us to that farther shore,
And long white shining lines of bones,
Make needless sign or white mile-stones.

The wild man's yell, the groaning wheel;
The train that moved like drifting barge;
The dust that rose up like a cloud,
Like smoke of distant battle! Loud
The great whips rang like shot, and steel
Of antique fashion, crude and large,
Flash'd back as in some battle charge.

They sought, yea, they did find their rest
Along that long and lonesome way,
These brave men buffeting the West
With lifted faces.
Full were they
Of great endeavor. Brave and true
As stern Crusader clad in steel,
They died a-field as it was fit.
Made strong with hope, they dared to do
Achievement that a host to-day
Would stagger at, stand back and reel,
Defeated at the thought of it.

What brave endeavor to endure!
What patient hope, when hope was past!
What still surrender at the last,
A thousand leagues from hope! how pure
They lived, how proud they died!
How generous with life!
The wide
And gloried age of chivalry
Hath not one page like this to me.

Let all these golden days go by,
In sunny summer weather. I
But think upon my buried brave,
And breathe beneath another sky.
Let beauty glide in gilded car,
And find my sundown seas afar,
Forgetful that 'tis but one grave
From eastmost to the westmost wave.

Yea, I remember! The still tears

That o'er uncoffin'd faces fell!
The final, silent, sad farewell!
God! these are with me all the years!
They shall be with me ever. I
Shall not forget. I hold a trust.
They are a part of my existence.
When
Adown the shining iron track
You sweep, and fields of corn flash back,
And herds of lowing steers move by,
And men laugh loud, in mute distrust,
I turn to other days, to men
Who made a pathway with their dust.

XV.

At last he pass'd all men or sign
Of man. Yet still his long black line
Was push'd and pointed for the west;
The sea, the utmost sea, and rest.

He climbed, descended, climbed again,
Until he stood at last as lone,
As solitary and unknown,
As some lost ship upon the main.

O there was grandeur in his air,
An old-time splendor in his eye,
When he had climb'd the bleak, the high,
The rock-built bastions of the plain,
And thrown a-back his blown white hair,
And halting turn'd to look again.

And long, from out his lofty place,
He look'd far down the fading plain
For his pursuers, but in vain.
Yea, he was glad. Across his face
A careless smile was seen to play,
The first for many a stormy day.

He turn'd to Ina, dark and fair
As some sad twilight; touch'd her hair,
Stoop'd low, and kiss'd her silently,
Then silent held her to his breast.
Then waved command to his black men,
Look'd east, then mounted slow, and then
Led leisurely against the west.

And why should he, who dared to die,
Who more than once with hissing breath
Had set his teeth and pray'd for death,
Have fled these men, or wherefore fly
Before them now? why not defy?

His midnight men were strong and true,
And not unused to strife, and knew
The masonry of steel right well,
And all its signs that lead to hell.

It might have been his youth had wrought
Some wrong his years would now repair
That made him fly and still forbear;
It might have been he only sought
To lead them to some fatal snare
And let them die by piece-meal there.

It might have been that his own blood,
A brother, son, pursued with curse.
It might have been this woman fair
Was this man's child, an only thing
To love in all the universe,
And that the old man's iron will
Kept pirate's child from pirate still.
These rovers had a world their own,
Had laws, lived lives, went ways unknown.

I trow it was not shame or fear
Of any man or any thing
That death in any shape might bring.
It might have been some lofty sense
Of his own truth and innocence,
And virtues lofty and severe —
Nay, nay! what need of reasons here?

They touch'd a fringe of tossing trees
That bound a mountain's brow like bay,
And through the fragrant boughs a breeze
Blew salt-flood freshness.
Far away,
From mountain brow to desert base
Lay chaos, space, unbounded space,
In one vast belt of purple bound.
The black men cried, "The sea!" They bow'd
Their black heads in their hard black hands.
They wept for joy.

They laugh'd, and broke
The silence of an age, and spoke
Of rest at last; and, group'd in bands,
They threw their long black arms about
Each other's necks, and laugh'd aloud,
Then wept again with laugh and shout.

Yet Morgan spake no word, but led
His band with oft-averted head
Right through the cooling trees, till he
Stood out upon the lofty brow
And mighty mountain wall.
And now
The men who shouted, "Lo, the sea!"
Rode in the sun; but silently:
Stood in the sun, then look'd below.
They look'd but once, then look'd away,
Then look'd each other in the face.
They could not lift their brows, nor say,
But held their heads, nor spake, for lo!

Nor sea, nor voice of sea, nor breath
Of sea, but only sand and death,
And one eternity of space
Confronted them with fiery face.

'Twas vastness even as a sea,
So still it sang in symphonies;
But yet without the sense of seas,
Save depth, and space, and distances.
'Twas all so shoreless, so profound,
It seem'd it were earth's utter bound.
'Twas like the dim edge of death is,
'Twas hades, hell, eternity!

XVI.

THEN Morgan hesitating stood,
Look'd down the deep and steep descent
With wilder'd brow and wonderment,
Then gazed against the cooling wood.

And she beside him gazed at this,
Then turn'd her great, sad eyes to his;
He shook his head and look'd away,
Then sadly smiled, and still did say,
"To-morrow, child, another day."

O thou to-morrow! Mystery!
O day that ever runs before!
What has thine hidden hand in store
For mine, to-morrow, and for me?
O thou to-morrow! what hast thou
In store to make me bear the now?

O day in which we shall forget
The tangled troubles of to-day!
O day that laughs at duns, at debt!
O day of promises to pay!
O shelter from all present storm!
O day in which we shall reform!

O day of all days for reform!
Convenient day of promises!
Hold back the shadow of the storm.
O bless'd to-morrow! Chiefest friend,
Let not thy mystery be less,
But lead us blindfold to the end.

XVII.

Old Morgan eyed his men, look'd back
Against the groves of tamarack,
Then tapp'd his stirrup-foot, and stray'd
His hard left hand along the mane
Of his strong steed, and careless play'd
His fingers through the silken skein,
And seemed a time to touch the rein.

And then he spurr'd him to her side,
And reach'd his hand and, leaning wide,
He smiling push'd her falling hair
Back from her brow, and kiss'd her there.

Yea, touch'd her softly, as if she
Had been some priceless, tender flower,

Yet touch'd her as one taking leave
Of his one love in lofty tower
Before descending to the sea
Of battle on his battle eve.

XVIII.

A DISTANT shout! quick oaths! alarms!
The black men start up suddenly,
Stand in the stirrup, clutch their arms,
And bare bright arms all instantly.

But he, he slowly turns, and he
Looks all his full soul in her face.
He does not shout, he does not say,
But sits serenely in his place
A time, then slowly turns, looks back
Between the trim-bough'd tamarack,
And up the winding mountain way,
To where the long strong grasses lay.

He raised his glass in his two hands,
Then in his left hand let it fall,

Then seem'd to count his fingers o'er,
Then reach'd his glass, waved cold commands,
Then tapp'd his stirrup as before,
Stood in the stirrup stern and tall,
Then ran his hand along the mane
Half nervous-like, and that was all.

His head half settled on his breast,
His face a-beard like bird a-nest,
And then he roused himself, he spoke,
He reach'd an arm like arm of oak,
He struck a-west his great broad hand,
And seem'd to hurl his hot command.

He clutch'd his rein, struck sharp his heel,
Look'd at his men, and smiled half sad,
Half desperate, then hitch'd his steel,
And all his stormy presence had,
As if he kept once more his keel
On listless seas where breakers reel.

He toss'd again his iron hand
Above the deep, steep desert space,
Above the burning seas of sand,
And look'd his black men in the face.

They spake not, nor look'd back again,
They struck the heel, they clutch'd the rein,
And down the darkling plunging steep
They dropped toward the dried-up deep.

Below! It seem'd a league below,
The black men rode, and she rode well,
Against the gleaming sheening haze
That shone like some vast sea ablaze,
That seem'd to gleam, to glint, to glow
As if it mark'd the shores of hell.

Then Morgan stood alone, look'd back
From off the fierce wall where he stood,
And watch'd his dusk approaching foe.

He saw him creep along his track,
Saw him descending from the wood,
And smiled to see how worn and slow.

Then when his foemen hounding came
In pistol-shot of where he stood,
He wound his hand in his steed's mane,
And plunging to the desert plain,
Threw back his white beard like a cloud,
And looking back did shout aloud
Defiance like a stormy flood,
And shouted, "Vasques!" called his name,
And dared him to the desert flame.

XIX.

A CLOUD of dust adown the steep,
Where scarce a whirling hawk would sweep,
The cloud his foes had follow'd fast,
And Morgan like a cloud had pass'd,
Yet passed like some proud king of old;
And now mad Vasques could not hold
Control of his one wild desire
To meet old Morgan, in his ire.

He cursed aloud, he shook his rein
Above the desert darkling deep,
And urged his steed toward the steep,
But urged his weary steed in vain.

Old Morgan heard his oath and shout,
And Morgan turn'd his head once more,

And wheel'd his stout steed short about,
Then seem'd to count their numbers o'er.

And then his right hand touch'd his steel,
And then he tapp'd his iron heel
And seem'd to fight with thought.
At last,
As if the final die was cast,
And cast as carelessly as one
Would toss a white coin in the sun,
He touch'd his rein once more, and then
His pistol laid with idle heed
Prone down the toss'd mane of his steed,
And he rode down the rugged way
Tow'rd where the wide, white desert lay,
By broken gorge and cavern'd den,
And join'd his band of midnight men.

Some say the gray old man had crazed

From mountain fruits that he had pluck'd
While winding through the wooded ways
Above the steep.
But others say
That he had turn'd aside and suck'd
Sweet poison from the honey dews
That lie like manna all the day
On dewy leaves so crystal fair
And temptingly that none refuse ;
That thus made mad the man did dare
Confront the desert and despair.

Then other mountain men explain,
That when one looks upon this sea
Of glowing sand, he looks again,
Again, through gossamers that run
In scintillations of the sun
Along this white eternity,
And looks until the brain is dazed,
Bewilder'd, and the man is crazed.

Then one, a grizzled mountaineer,
A thin and sinewy old man,
With face all wrinkle-wrought, and tan,
And presence silent and austere,
Does tell a tale, with reaching face
And bated breath, of this weird place,
Of many a stalwart mountaineer
And Piute tall who perish'd here.

He tells a tale with whisper'd breath
Of skin-clad men who track'd this shore,
Once populous with sea-set town,
And saw a woman wondrous fair,
And, wooing, follow'd her far down
Through burning sands to certain death;
And then he catches short his breath.

He tells: Nay, this is all too long;
Enough. The old man shakes his hair
When he is done, and shuts his eyes,

So satisfied and so self-wise,
As if to say, " 'Tis nothing rare,
This following the luring fair
To death, and bound in thorny thong;
'Twas ever thus; the old, old song."

XX.

Go ye and look upon that land,
That far vast land that few behold,
And none beholding understand, —
That old, old land which men call new,
That land as old as time is old ; —
Go journey with the seasons through
Its wastes, and learn how limitless,
How shoreless lie the distances,
Before you come to question this
Or dare to dream what grandeur is.

The solemn silence of that plain,
Where unmanned tempests ride and reign,
It awes and it possesses you.
'Tis, oh! so eloquent.
The blue

And bended skies seem built for it,
With rounded roof all fashioned fit,
And frescoed clouds, quaint-wrought and true;
While all else seems so far, so vain,
An idle tale but illy told,
Before this land so lone and old.

Its story is of God alone,
For man has lived and gone away,
And left but little heaps of stone,
And all seems some long yesterday.

Lo! here you learn how more than fit
And dignified is silence, when
You hear the petty jeers of men
Who point, and show their pointless wit.

The vastness of that voiceless plain,
Its awful solitudes remain
Thenceforth for aye a part of you,

And you are of the favored few,
For you have learn'd your littleness,
And heed not names that name you less.

Some silent red men cross your track;
Some sun-tann'd trappers come and go;
Some rolling seas of buffalo
Break thunder-like and far away
Against the foot-hills, breaking back
Like breakers of some troubled bay;
But not a voice the long, lone day.

Some white-tail'd antelope blow by
So airy-like; some foxes shy
And shadow-like shoot to and fro
Like weavers' shuttles, as you pass;
And now and then from out the grass
You hear some lone bird cluck, and call
A sharp keen call for her lost brood,
That only makes the solitude,

That mantles like some sombre pall,
Seem deeper still, and that is all.

A wide domain of mysteries
And signs that men misunderstand!
A land of space and dreams; a land
Of sea-salt lakes and dried-up seas!

A land of caves and caravans,
And lonely wells and pools;
A land
That hath its purposes and plans,
That seems so like dead Palestine,
Save that its wastes have no confine
Till push'd against the levell'd skies;
A land from out whose depths shall rise
The new-time prophets.
Yea, the land
From out whose awful depths shall come,
All clad in skins, with dusty feet,

A man fresh from his Maker's hand,
A singer singing oversweet,
A charmer charming very wise ;
And then all men shall not be dumb.

Nay, not be dumb, for he shall say,
"Take heed, for I prepare the way
For weary feet."
                    Lo ! from this land
Of Jordan streams and sea-wash'd sand,
The Christ shall come when next the race
Of man shall look upon his face.

XXI.

Pursuer and pursued! who knows
The why he left the breezy pine,
The fragrant tamarack and vine,
Red rose and precious yellow rose!

Nay, Vasques held the vantage ground
Above him by the wooded steep,
And right nor left no passage lay,
And there was left him but that way,—
The way through blood, or to the deep
And lonesome deserts far profound,
That know not sight of man, or sound.

Hot Vasques stood upon the rim,
High, bold, and fierce with crag and spire.
He saw a far gray eagle swim,

He saw a black hawk wheel, retire,
And shun that desert wide a-wing,
But saw no other living thing.

High in the full sun's gold and flame
He halting and half waiting came
And stood below the belt of wood,
Then moved along the broken hill
And looked below.
And long he stood
With lips set firm and brow a-frown,
And warring with his iron will.
He mark'd the black line winding down
As if into the doors of death.
And as he gazed a breath arose
As from his far-retreating foes,
So hot it almost took his breath.

His black eye flashed an angry fire,
He stood upon the mountain brow,

With lifted arm like oaken bough;
The hot pursuer halting stood
Irresolute, in nettled ire;
Then look'd against the cooling wood,
Then strode he sullen to and fro,
Then turned and long he gazed below.

The sands flash'd back like fields of snow,
Like far blown seas that flood and flow.
The while the rounded sky rose higher,
And cleaving through the upper space,
The flush'd sun settled to his place,
Like some far hemisphere of fire.

And yet again he gazed. And now,
Far off and faint, he saw or guess'd
He saw, beyond the sands a-west,
A dim and distant lifting beach
That daring men might dare and reach:
Dim shapes of toppled peaks with pine,

And water'd foot-hills dark like wine,
And fruits on many a bended bough.

The leader turn'd and shook his head.
"And shall we turn aside," he said,
"Or dare this hell?" The men stood still
As leaning on his sterner will.

And then he stopp'd and turn'd again,
And held his broad hand to his brow,
And looked intent and eagerly.
The far white levels of the plain
Flash'd back like billows.
Even now
He saw rise up remote, 'mid sea,
'Mid space, 'mid wastes, 'mid nothingness,
A ship becalm'd as in distress.

The dim sign pass'd as suddenly,
A gossamer of golden tress,

Thrown over some still middle sea,
And then his eager eyes grew dazed, —
He brought his two hands to his face.
Again he raised his head, and gazed
With flashing eyes and visage fierce
Far out, and resolute to pierce
The far, far, faint receding reach
Of space and touch its farther beach.
He saw but space, unbounded space;
Eternal space and nothingness.

Then all wax'd anger'd as they gazed
Far out upon the shoreless land,
And clench'd their doubled hands and raised
Their long bare arms, but utter'd not.
At last one started from the band,
His bosom heaved as billows heave,
Great heaving bosom, broad and brown:
He raised his arm, push'd up his sleeve,
Push'd bare his arm, strode up and down,

With hat pushed back, and flushed and
hot,
And shot sharp oaths like cannon shot.

Again the man stood still, again
He strode the height like hoary storm,
Then shook his fists, and then his form
Did writhe as if it writhed with pain.

And yet again his face was raised,
And yet again he gazed and gazed,
Above his fading, failing foe,
With gather'd brow and visage fierce,
As if his soul would part or pierce
The awful depths that lay below.

He had as well look'd on that sea
That keeps Samoa's coral isles
Amid ten thousand watery miles,
Bound round by one eternity ;

Bound round by realms of nothingness,
In love with their own loneliness.
He saw but space, unbounded space,
And brought his brown hands to his face.

There roll'd away to left, to right,
Unbroken walls as black as night,
And back of these there distant rose
Steep cones of everlasting snows.

At last he was resolved, his form
Seem'd like a pine blown rampt with storm.
He mounted, clutch'd his reins, and then
Turn'd sharp and savage to his men;
And silent then led down the way
To night that knows not night nor day.

XXII.

LIKE some great serpent black and still,
Old Morgan's men stole down the hill.
Far down the steep they wound and wound
Until the black line touched that land
Of gleaming white and silver sand
That knows not human sight or sound.

How broken plunged the steep descent;
How barren! Desolate, and rent
By earthquake's shock, the land lay dead,
With dust and ashes on its head.

'Twas as some old world overthrown,
Where Theseus fought and Sappho dreamed
In eons ere they touched this land,
And found their proud souls foot and hand
Bound to the flesh and stung with pain.

An ugly skeleton it seem'd
Of its own self. The fiery rain
Of red volcanoes here had sown
The death of cities of the plain.

The very devastation gleamed.
All burnt and black, and rent and seam'd,
Ay, vanquished quite and overthrown,
And torn with thunder-stroke, and strown
With cinders, lo! the dead earth lay
As waiting for the judgment day.

Why, tamer men had turn'd and said,
On seeing this, with start and dread,
And whisper'd each with gather'd breath,
"We come on the confines of death."

They wound below a savage bluff
That lifted, from its sea-mark'd base,
Great walls with characters cut rough

And deep by some long-perish'd race;
And lo! strange beasts unnamed, unknown,
Stood hewn and limn'd upon the stone.

The iron hoofs sank here and there,
Plough'd deep in ashes, broke anew
Old broken idols, and laid bare
Old bits of vessels that had grown,
As countless ages cycled through,
Imbedded with the common stone.

A mournful land as land can be
Beneath their feet in ashes lay,
Beside that dread and dried-up sea;
A city older than that gray
And grass-grown tower builded when
Confusion cursed the tongues of men.

Beneath, before, a city lay
That in her majesty had shamed

The wolf-nursed conqueror of old;
Below, before, and far away
There reach'd the white arm of a bay,
A broad bay shrunk to sand and stone,
Where ships had rode and breakers roll'd
When Babylon was yet unnamed,
And Nimrod's hunting-fields unknown.

Some serpents slid from out the grass
That grew in tufts by shatter'd stone,
Then hid beneath some broken mass
That Time had eaten as a bone
Is eaten by some savage beast;
An everlasting palace feast.

A dull-eyed rattlesnake that lay
All loathsome, yellow-skinn'd, and slept,
Coil'd tight as pine-knot, in the sun,
With flat head through the centre run,
Struck blindly back, then rattling crept

Flat-bellied down the dusty way . . .
'Twas all the dead land had to say.

Two pink-eyed hawks, wide-wing'd and gray,
Scream'd savagely, and, circling high,
And screaming still in mad dismay,
Grew dim and died against the sky . . .
'Twas all the heavens had to say.

The grasses fail'd, and then a mass
Of brown, burnt cactus ruled the land,
And topt the hillocks of hot sand,
Where scarce the hornèd toad could pass.
Then stunted sage on either hand,
All loud with odors, spread the land.

The sun rose right above, and fell
As falling molten as they pass'd.
Some low-built junipers at last,
The last that o'er the desert look'd,

Thick-bough'd, and black as shapes of hell
Where dumb owls sat with bent bills hook'd
Beneath their wings awaiting night,
Rose up, then faded from the sight:
Then not another living thing
Crept on the sand or kept the wing.

White Azteckee! Dead Azteckee!
Vast sepulchre of buried sea!
What dim ghosts hover on thy rim,
What stately-manner'd shadows swim
Along thy gleaming waste of sands
And shoreless limits of dead lands?

Dread Azteckee! Dead Azteckee!
White place of ghosts, give up thy dead:
Give back to Time thy buried hosts!
The new world's tawny Ishmaelite,
The roving tent-born Shoshonee,
Who shuns thy shores as death, at night,

Because thou art so white, so dread,
Because thou art so ghostly white,
Because thou hast thy buried hosts,
Has named thy shores "the place of ghosts."

Thy white uncertain sands are white
With bones of thy unburied dead
That will not perish from the sight.
They drown but perish not, — ah me!
What dread unsightly sights are spread
Along this lonesome dried-up sea.

White Azteckee, give up to me
Of all thy prison'd dead but one,
That now lies bleaching in the sun,
To tell what strange allurements lie
Within this dried-up oldest sea,
To tempt men to its heart and die.

Old, hoar, and dried-up sea! so old!
So strewn with wealth, so sown with gold!

Yea, thou art old and hoary white
With time, and ruin of all things;
And on thy lonesome borders night
Sits brooding as with wounded wings.

The winds that toss'd thy waves and blew
Across thy breast the blowing sail,
And cheer'd the hearts of cheering crew
From farther seas, no more prevail.

Thy white-wall'd cities all lie prone,
With but a pyramid, a stone,
Set head and foot in sands to tell
The tired stranger where they fell.

The patient ox that bended low
His neck, and drew slow up and down
Thy thousand freights through rock-built town
Is now the free-born buffalo.

No longer of the timid fold,

The mountain sheep leaps free and bold
His high-built summit and looks down
From battlements of buried town.

Thine ancient steeds know not the rein;
They lord the land; they come, they go
At will; they laugh at man; they blow
A cloud of black steeds o'er the plain.

Thy monuments lie buried now,
The ashes whiten on thy brow,
The winds, the waves, have drawn away,
The very wild man dreads to stay.

O! thou art very old. I lay,
Made dumb with awe and wonderment,
Beneath a palm before my tent,
With idle and discouraged hands,
Not many days agone, on sands
Of awful, silent Africa.

Long gazing on her mighty shades,
I did recall a semblance there
Of thee. I mused where story fades
From her dark brow and found her fair.

A slave, and old, within her veins
There runs that warm, forbidden blood
That no man dares to dignify
In elevated song.

The chains
That held her race but yesterday
Hold still the hands of men. Forbid
Is Ethiop.

The turbid flood
Of prejudice lies stagnant still,
And all the world is tainted. Will
And wit lie broken as a lance
Against the brazen mailed face
Of old opinion.

None advance
Steel-clad and glad to the attack,
With trumpet and with song. Look back!
Beneath yon pyramids lie hid
The histories of her great race.
Old Nilus rolls right sullen by,
With all his secrets.

Who shall say:
My father rear'd a pyramid;
My brother clipp'd the dragon's wings;
My mother was Semiramis?
Yea, harps strike idly out of place;
Men sing of savage Saxon kings
New-born and known but yesterday,
And Norman blood presumes to say. . . .

Nay, ye who boast ancestral name
And vaunt deeds dignified by time
Must not despise her.

Who hath worn
Since time began a face that is
So all-enduring, old like this —
A face like Africa's?

Behold!
The Sphinx is Africa. The bond
Of silence is upon her.

Old
And white with tombs, and rent and
shorn;
With raiment wet with tears, and torn,
And trampled on, yet all untamed;
All naked now, yet not ashamed, —
The mistress of the young world's prime,
Whose obelisks still laugh at Time,
And lift to heaven her fair name,
Sleeps satisfied upon her fame.

Beyond the Sphinx, and still beyond,
Beyond the tawny desert-tomb

Of Time ; beyond tradition, loom
And lift ghostlike from out the gloom
Her thousand cities, battle-torn
And gray with story and with time.
Her very ruins are sublime,
Her thrones with mosses overborne
Make velvets for the feet of Time.

She points a hand and cries : " Go read
The letter'd obelisks that lord
Old Rome, and know my name and deed.
My archives these, and plunder'd when
I had grown weary of all men."
We turn to these ; we cry : "Abhorr'd
Old Sphinx, behold, we cannot read ! "

And yet my dried-up desert sea
Was populous with blowing sail,
And set with city, white-wall'd town,
All mann'd with armies bright with mail,

Ere yet that awful Sphinx sat down
To gaze into eternity,
Or Egypt knew her natal hour,
Or Africa had name or power.

XXIII.

AWAY upon the sandy seas,
The gleaming, burning, boundless plain.
How solemn-like, how still, as when
The mighty-minded Genoese
Drew three tall ships and led his men
From land they might not meet again.

The black men rode in front by two,
The fair one follow'd close, and kept
Her face held down as if she wept ;
But Morgan kept the rear, and threw
His flowing, swaying beard aback
Anon along their lonesome track.

They rode against the level sun,
And spake not he or any one.

The weary day fell down to rest,
A star upon his mantled breast,
Ere scarce the sun fell out of space,
And Venus glimmer'd in his place.

. . . .

Yea, all the stars shone just as fair,
And constellations kept their round,
And look'd from out the great profound,
And marched, and countermarch'd, and shone
Upon that desolation there,
Why just the same as if proud man
Strode up and down array'd in gold
And purple as in days of old,
And reckon'd all of his own plan,
Or made at least for man alone
And man's dominion from a throne.

Yet on push'd Morgan silently,
And straight as strong ship on a sea;
And ever as he rode there lay

To right, to left, and in his way,
Strange objects looming in the dark,
Some like a mast, or ark, or bark.

And things half hidden in the sand
Lay down before them where they pass'd, —
A broken beam, half-buried mast,
A spar or bar, such as might be
Blown crosswise, tumbled on the strand
Of some sail-crowded stormy sea.

XXIV.

All night by moon, by morning star,
The still, black men still kept their way;
All night till morn, till burning day,
Hot Vasques follow'd fast and far.

The sun shot arrows instantly;
And men turn'd east against the sun,
And men did look and cry, "The sea!"
And Morgan look'd, nay, every one
Did look, and lift his hand, and shade
His brow and look, and look dismay'd.

Lo! looming up before the sun,
Before their eyes, yet far away,
A ship with many a tall mast lay,—
Lay resting, as if she had run

Some splendid race through seas, and won
The right to rest in salt flood bay,—
And lay until the level sun
Uprose, and then she fell away,
As mists melt in the full of day.

Old Morgan lifts his bony hand,
He does not speak or make command,—
Short time for wonder, doubt, delay;
Dark objects sudden heave in sight
As if blown out or born of night.
It is enough, they turn; away!

The sun is high, the sands are hot
To touch, and all the tawny plain,
That glistens white with salt sea sand,
Sinks white and open as they tread
And trudge, with half-averted head,
As if to swallow them amain.
They look, as men look back to land

When standing out to stormy sea,
But still keep face and murmur not;
Keep stern and still as destiny,
Or iron king of Germany.

It was a sight! A slim dog slid
White-mouth'd and still along the sand,
The pleading picture of distress.
He stopp'd, leap'd up to lick a hand,
A hard black hand that sudden chid
Him back and check'd his tenderness;
But when the black man turn'd his head
His poor mute friend had fallen dead.

The very air hung white with heat,
And white, and fair, and far away
A lifted, shining snow-shaft lay
As if to mock their mad retreat.

The white, salt sands beneath their feet

Did make the black men loom as grand,
From out the lifting, heaving heat,
As they rode sternly on and on,
As any bronze men in the land
That sit their statue steeds upon.

The men were silent as men dead.
The sun hung centred overhead,
Nor seem'd to move. It molten hung
Like some great central burner swung
From lofty beams with golden bars
In sacristy set round with stars.

XXV.

WHY, flame could hardly be more hot;
Yet on the mad pursuer came,
Across the gleaming yielding ground,
Right on, as if he fed on flame,
Right on until the mid-day found
The man within a pistol-shot.

He hail'd, but Morgan answer'd not,
He hail'd, then came a feeble shot,
And strangely, in that vastness there,
It seem'd to scarcely fret the air,
But fell down harmless anywhere.

He fiercely hail'd; and then there fell
A horse. And then a man fell down,
And in the sea-sand seem'd to drown.

Then Vasques cursed, but scarce could tell
The sound of his own voice, and all
In mad confusion seem'd to fall.

Yet on push'd Morgan, silent on,
And as he rode he lean'd and drew,
From his catenas, gold, and threw
The bright coins in the glaring sun.
But Vasques did not heed a whit,
He scarcely deign'd to scowl at it.

Again lean'd Morgan! He uprose,
And held a high hand to his foes,
And held two goblets up, and one
Did shine as if itself a sun.

Then leaning backward from his place,
He hurl'd them in his foemen's face,
Then drew again, and so kept on,
Till goblets, gold, and all were gone.

Yea, strew'd them out upon the sands
As men upon a frosty morn,
In Mississippi's fertile lands,
Hurl out great, yellow ears of corn
To hungry swine with hurried hands,

XXVI.

Lo! still hot Vasques urges on,
With flashing eye and flushing cheek.
What would he have? what does he seek?
He does not heed the gold a whit,
He does not deign to look at it;
But now his gleaming steel is drawn,
And now he leans, would hail again,—
He opes his swollen lips in vain.

But look you! See! A lifted hand,
And Vasques beckons his command.
He cannot speak, he leans, and he
Bends low upon his saddle-bow.
And now his blade drops to his knee,
And now he falters, now comes on,

And now his head is bended low ;
And now his rein, his steel, is gone ;
Now faint as any child is he,
And now his steed sinks to the knee.

XXVII.

The sun hung molten in mid space,
Like some great star fix'd in its place.
From out the gleaming spaces rose
A sheen of gossamer and danced,
As Morgan slow and still advanced
Before his far-receding foes.

Right on and on the still black line
Drove straight through gleaming sand and
shine,
By spar and beam and mast and stray,
And waif of sea and cast-away.

The far peaks faded from their sight,
The mountain walls fell down like night,
And nothing now was to be seen

Save but the dim sun hung in sheen
Of fairy garments all blood-red, —
The hell beneath, the hell o'erhead.

A black man tumbled from his steed.
He clutch'd in death the moving sands.
He caught the round earth in his hands,
He gripp'd it, held it hard and grim. . . .
The great sad mother did not heed
His hold, but pass'd right on from him,
And ere he died grew far and dim.

XXVIII.

The sun seem'd broken loose at last,
And settled slowly to the west,
Half hidden as he fell a-rest,
Yet, like the flying Parthian, cast
His keenest arrows as he pass'd.

On, on, the black men slowly drew
Their length, like some great serpent through
The sands, and left a hollow'd groove:
They march'd, they scarcely seem'd to move.
How patient in their muffled tread!
How like the dead march of the dead!

At last the slow black line was check'd,
An instant only; now again
It moved, it falter'd now, and now

It settled in its sandy bed,
And steeds stood rooted to the plain.
Then all stood still, and men somehow
Look'd down and with averted head;
Look'd down, nor dared look up, nor reck'd
Of any thing, of ill or good,
But bowed and stricken still they stood.

Like some brave band that dared the fierce
And bristled steel of gather'd host,
These daring men had dared to pierce
This awful vastness, dead and gray.
And now at last brought well at bay
They stood, — but each stood to his post;
Each man an unencompassed host.

Then one dismounted, waved a hand,
'Twas Morgan's stern and still command.
There fell a clash, like loosen'd chain,
And men dismounting loosed the rein.

Then every steed stood loosed and free ;
And some stepp'd slow and mute aside,
And some sank to the sands and died,
And some stood still as shadows be,
And men stood gazing silently.

XXIX.

OLD Morgan turn'd and raised his hand,
And laid it level with his eyes,
And look'd far back along the land.
He saw a dark dust still uprise,
Still surely tend to where he lay.
He did not curse, he did not say,
He did not even look surprise,
But silent turned to her his eyes.

Nay, he was over-gentle now,
He wiped a time his Titan brow,
Then sought dark Ina in her place,
Put out his arms, put down his face
And look'd in hers.

She reach'd her hands,
She lean'd, she fell upon his breast ;

He reach'd his arms around ; she lay
As lies a bird in leafy nest.
And he look'd out across the sands,
And then his face fell down, he smiled,
And softly said, " My child, my child ! "
Then bent his head and strode away.

And as he strode he turn'd his head,
He sidewise cast his brief commands ;
He led right on across the sands.
They rose and follow'd where he led.

XXX.

'TWAS so like night, the sun was dim,
Some black men settled down to rest,
But none made murmur or request.
The dead were dead, and that were best;
The living leaning follow'd him,
In huddled heaps, half nude, and grim.

The day through high mid-heaven rode
Across the sky, the dim red day;
Awest the warlike day-god strode
With shoulder'd shield away, away.

The savage, warlike day bent low,
As reapers bend in gathering grain,
As archer bending bends yew bow,
And flush'd and fretted as in pain.

Then down his shoulder slid his shield,
So huge, so awful, so blood-red
And batter'd as from battle-field :
It settled, sunk to his left hand,
Sunk down and down, it touch'd the sand,
Then day along the land lay dead,
Without one candle at his head.

XXXI.

AND now the moon wheel'd white and vast,
A round, unbroken, marbled moon,
And touch'd the far bright buttes of snow,
Then climb'd their shoulders over soon;
And there she seem'd to sit at last,
To hang, to hover there, to grow,
Grow vaster than vast peaks of snow.

Grow whiter than the snow's own breast,
Grow softer than September's noon,
Until the snow-peaks seem'd at best
But one wide, shining, shatter'd moon.

She sat the battlements of time;
She shone in mail of frost and rime,

A time, and then rose up and stood
In heaven in sad widowhood.

. . . .

The faded moon fell wearily,
And then the sun right suddenly
Rose up full arm'd, and rushing came
Across the land like flood of flame.

XXXII.

THE sun roll'd on. Lo! hills uprose
As push'd against the arching skies, —
As if to meet the timid sun —
Rose sharp from out the sultry dun,
Set well with wood, and brier, and rose,
And seem'd to hold the free repose
Of lands where rocky summits rise,
Or unfenced fields of Paradise.

The black men look'd up from the sands
Against the dim, uncertain skies,
As men that disbelieved their eyes,
And would have laugh'd; they wept in-
stead,
With shoulders heaved, with bowing head
Hid down between their two black hands.

They stood and gazed. Lo! like the call
Of spring-time promises, the trees
Lean'd from their lifted mountain wall,
And stood clear cut against the skies
As if they grew in pistol-shot.
Yet all the mountains answer'd not,
And yet there came no cooling breeze,
Nor soothing sense of windy trees.

At last old Morgan, looking through
His shaded fingers, let them go,
And let his load fall down as dead.
He groan'd, he clutch'd his beard of snow
As was his wont, then bowing low,
Took up his life, and moaning said,
"Lord Christ! 'tis the mirage, and we
Stand blinded in a burning sea."

O sweet deceit when minds despair!
O mad deceit of man betray'd!

O mother Nature, thou art fair,
But thou art false as man or maid.

Yea, many lessons, mother Earth,
Have we thy children learn'd of thee
In sweet deceit. . . . The sudden birth
Of hope that dies mocks destiny.

O mother Earth, thy promises
Are fallen leaves; they lie forgot!
Such lessons! How could we learn less?
We are but children, blame us not.

XXXIII.

AGAIN they move, but where or how
It recks them little, nothing now.
Yet Morgan leads them as before,
But totters now; he bends, and he
Is like a broken ship a-sea, —
A ship that knows not any shore,
And knows it shall not anchor more.

Some leaning shadows crooning crept
Through desolation, crown'd in dust.
And had the mad pursuer kept
His path, and cherished his pursuit?
There lay no choice. Advance he must:
Advance, and eat his ashen fruit.

Yet on, and on old Morgan led.

His black men totter'd to and fro,
A leaning, huddled heap of woe;
Then one fell down, then two fell dead;
Yet not one moaning word was said.

They made no sign, they said no word,
Nor lifted once black, helpless hands;
And all the time no sound was heard
Save but the dull, dead, muffled tread
Of shuffled feet in shining sands.

Again the still moon rose and stood
Above the dim, dark belt of wood,
Above the buttes, above the snow,
And bent a sad, sweet face below.

She reach'd along the level plain
Her long, white fingers. Then again
She reach'd, she touch'd the snowy sands,
Then reach'd far out until she touch'd

A heap that lay with doubled hands,
Reach'd from its sable self, and clutch'd
With death.
                    O tenderly
That black, that dead and hollow face
Was kiss'd at midnight. . . .
                                        What if I say
The long, white moonbeams reaching there,
Caressing idle hands of clay,
And resting on the wrinkled hair
And great lips push'd in sullen pout,
Were God's own fingers reaching out
From heaven to that lonesome place?

XXXIV.

By waif and stray and cast-away,
Such as are seen in seas withdrawn,
Old Morgan led in silence on,
And sometime lifting up his head
To guide his footsteps as he led,
He deem'd he saw a great ship lay
Her keel along the sea-wash'd sand,
As with her captain's old command.

. . . .

The stars were seal'd ; and then a haze
Of gossamer fill'd all the west,
So like in Indian summer days,
And veil'd all things.

And then the moon
Grew pale, and faint, and far. She died,

And now nor star nor any sign
Fell out of heaven.
Oversoon
Some black men fell. Then at their side
Some one sat down to watch, to rest . . .
To rest, to watch, or what you will,
The man sits resting, watching still.

XXXV.

THE day glared through the eastern rim
Of rocky peaks, as prison bars;
With light as dim as distant stars
The sultry sunbeams filter'd down
Through misty phantoms weird and dim,
Through shifting shapes bat-wing'd and
brown.

Like some vast ruin wrapp'd in flame
The sun fell down before them now.
Behind them wheel'd white peaks of snow,
As they proceeded.
Gray and grim
And awful objects went and came
Before them then. They pierced at last

The desert's middle depths, and lo!
There loom'd from out the desert vast
A lonely ship, well-built and trim,
And perfect all in hull and mast.

No storm had stain'd it any whit,
No seasons set their teeth in it.
Her masts were white as ghosts, and tall;
Her decks were as of yesterday.
The rains, the elements, and all
The moving things that bring decay
By fair green lands or fairer seas,
Had touch'd not here for centuries.

Lo! date had lost all reckoning,
And Time had long forgotten all
In this lost land, and no new thing
Or old could anywise befall,
Or morrows, or a yesterday,
For Time went by the other way.

The ages have not any course
Across this untrack'd waste.
The sky
Wears here one blue, unbending hue,
The heavens one unchanging mood.
The far still stars they filter through
The heavens, falling bright and bold
Against the sands as beams of gold.
The wide, white moon forgets her force;
The very sun rides round and high,
As if to shun this solitude.

What dreams of gold or conquest drew
The oak-built sea-king to these seas,
Ere Earth, old Earth, unsatisfied,
Rose up and shook man in disgust
From off her wearied breast, and threw
And smote his cities down, and dried
These measured, town-set seas to dust?
Who trod these decks?

What captain knew
The straits that led to lands like these?

Blew south-sea breeze or north-sea breeze?
What spiced winds whistled through this sail?
What banners stream'd above these seas?
And what strange seaman answer'd back
To other sea-king's beck and hail,
That blew across his foamy track!

Sought Jason here the golden fleece?
Came Trojan ship or ships of Greece?
Came decks dark-mann'd from sultry Ind,
Woo'd here by spacious wooing wind?
So like a grand, sweet woman, when
A great love moves her soul to men?

Came here strong ships of Solomon
In quest of Ophir by Cathay? . . .
Sit down and dream of seas withdrawn,

And every sea-breath drawn away. . . .
Sit down, sit down!
                                        What is the good
That we go on still fashioning
Great iron ships or walls of wood,
High masts of oak, or any thing?

Lo! all things moving must go by.
The sea lies dead. Behold, this land
Sits desolate in dust beside
His snow-white, seamless shroud of sand;
The very clouds have wept and died,
And only God is in the sky.

XXXVI.

THE sands lay heaved, as heaved by waves,
As fashion'd in a thousand graves:
And wrecks of storm blown here and there,
And dead men scatter'd everywhere;
And strangely clad they seem'd to be
Just as they sank in that old sea.

The mermaid with her splendid hair
Had clung about a wreck's beam there;
And sung her song of sweet despair,
The time she saw the seas withdrawn
And all her home and glory gone:

Had sung her melancholy dirge,
Above the last receding surge,
And, looking down the rippled tide,
Had sung, and with her song had died.

The monsters of the sea lay bound
In strange contortions. Coil'd around
A mast half heaved above the sand,
The great sea-serpent's folds were found,
As solid as ship's iron band.
And basking in the burning sun
There rose the great whale's skeleton.

A thousand sea things stretch'd across
Their weary and bewilder'd way:
Great unnamed monsters wrinkled lay
With sunken eyes and shrunken form.
The strong sea-horse that rode the storm
With mane as light and white as floss,
Lay tangled in his mane of moss.

And anchor, hull, and cast-away,
And all things that the miser deep
Doth in his darkling locker keep,
To right and left around them lay.

Yea, coins lay there on either hand,
Lay shining in the silver sand;
As plenty in the wide sands lay
As stars along the Milky Way.

And golden coin, and golden cup,
And golden cruse, and golden plate,
And all that great seas swallow up,
Right in their dreadful pathway lay. . . .
The hungry and insatiate
Old sea, made hoary white with time,
And wrinkled cross with many a crime,
With all his treasured thefts was there,
His sins, his very soul laid bare,
As if it were the Judgment Day.

XXXVII.

AND now the tawny night fell soon,
And there was neither star nor moon;
And yet it seem'd it was not night.
There fell a phosphorescent light,
There rose from white sands and dead
men
A soft light, white and fair as when
The Spirit of Jehovah moved
Upon the water's conscious face,
And made it His abiding-place.

O mighty waters unreproved!
Thou deep! where the Jehovah moved
Ere soul of man was called to be!

O seas! that were created not
As man, as earth, as light, as aught
That is. O sea! thou art to me
A terror, death, eternity.

XXXVIII.

I DO recall some sad days spent,
By borders of the Orient,
Days sweet as sad to memory . . .
'Twould make a tale. It matters not . . .
I sought the loneliest seas; I sought
The solitude of ruins, and forgot
Mine own lone life and littleness
Before this fair land's mute distress,
That sat within this changeful sea.

Slow sailing through the reedy isles,
By unknown banks, through unknown
bays,
Some sunny, summer yesterdays,

Where Nature's beauty still beguiles,
I saw the storied yellow sail
And lifted prow of steely mail.
'Tis all that's left Torcello now, —
A pirate's yellow sail, a prow.

Below the far, faint peaks of snow,
And grass-grown causeways well below,
I touched Torcello.
Once a-land,
I took a sea-shell in my hand,
And blew like any trumpeter.
I felt the fig-leaves lift and stir
On trees that reached from ruined wall
Above my head, but that was all.
Back from the farther island shore
Came echoes trooping; nothing more.

Lo! here stood Adria once, and here
Attila came with sword and flame,

And set his throne of hollowed stone
In her high mart.
And it remains
Still lord o'er all. Where once the tears
Of mute petition fell, the rains
Of heaven fall. Lo! all alone
There lifts this massive empty throne!
The sea has changed his meed, his mood,
And made this sedgy solitude.

By cattle paths grass-grown and worn,
Through marbled streets all stain'd and
torn
By time and battle, there I walked.
A bent old beggar, white as one
For better fruitage blossoming,
Came on. And as he came he talked
Unto himself; for there are none
In all his island, old and dim,
To answer back or question him.

I turned, retraced my steps once more.
The hot miasma steamed and rose
In deadly vapor from the reeds
That grew from out the shallow shore,
Where peasants say the sea-horse feeds,
And Neptune shapes his horn and blows.

I climb'd and sat that throne of stone
To contemplate, to dream, to reign;
Ay, reign above myself; to call
The people of the past again
Before me as I sat alone
In all my kingdom.
There were kine
That browsed along the reedy brine,
And now and then a tusky boar
Would shake the high reeds of the shore,
A bird blow by, — but that was all.

I watched the lonesome sea-gull pass.

I did remember and forget;
The past rolled by; I stood alone.
I sat the shapely chiselled stone
That stands in tall sweet grasses set;
Ay, girdle deep in long strong grass,
And green Alfalfa.
Very fair
The heavens were, and still and blue,
For Nature knows no changes there.
The Alps of Venice, far away
Like some half-risen half moon lay.

How sweet the grasses at my feet!
The smell of clover over sweet.
I heard the hum of bees. The bloom
Of clover-tops and cherry-trees
Were being rifled by the bees,
And these were building in a tomb.

The fair Alfalfa; such as has

Usurped the Occident, and grows
With all the sweetness of the rose
On Sacramento's sundown hills,
Is there, and that mid island fills
With fragrance. Yet the smell of death
Comes riding in on every breath.

Lo! death that is not death, but rest:
To step aside, to watch and wait
Beside the wave, outside the gate,
With all life's pulses in your breast:
To absolutely rest, to pray
In some lone mountain while you may.

That sad sweet fragrance. It had sense
And sound, and voice. It was a part
Of that which had possessed my heart,
And would not of my will go hence.
'Twas Autumn's breath; 'twas dear as kis
Of any worshipped woman is.

Some snails have climb'd the throne and writ
Their silver monograms on it
In unknown tongues.
I sat thereon,
I dreamed until the day was gone;
I blew again my pearly shell, —
Blew long and strong, and loud and well;
I puffed my cheeks, I blew, as when
Horn'd satyrs danced the delight of men.

Some mouse-brown cows that fed within
Looked up. A cowherd rose hard by,
My single subject, clad in skin,
Nor yet half clad. I caught his eye,
He stared at me, then turned and fled.
He frightened fled, and as he ran,
Like wild beast from the face of man,
Across his shoulder threw his head.
He gathered up his skin of goat
About his breast and hairy throat.

He stopped, and then this subject true,
Mine only one in lands like these
Made desolate by changeful seas,
Came back and asked me for a *sou*.

XXXIX.

AND yet again through the watery miles
Of reeds I rowed till the desolate isles
Of the black bead-makers of Venice are not.
I touched where a single sharp tower is shot
To heaven, and torn by thunder and rent
As if it had been Time's battlement.
A city lies dead, and this great gravestone
Stands at its head like a ghost alone.

Some cherry-trees grow here, and here
An old church, simple and severe
In ancient aspect, stands alone
Amid the ruin and decay, all grown
In moss and grasses.
Old and quaint,
With antique cuts of martyr'd saint,

The gray church stands with stooping knees,
Defying the decay of seas.

Her pictured Hell, with flames blown high,
In bright mosaics wrought and set
When man first knew the Nubian art,
Her bearded saints, as black as jet;
Her quaint Madonna, dim with rain
And touch of pious lips of pain,
So touched my lonesome soul, that I
Gazed long, then came and gazed again,
And loved, and took her to my heart.

Nor monk in black, nor Capuchin,
Nor priest of any creed was seen.
A sun-browned woman, old and tall,
And still as any shadow is,
Stole forth from out the mossy wall
With massive keys to show me this:
Came slowly forth, and following,
Three birds — and all with drooping wing.

Three mute brown babes of hers; and they —
O, they were beautiful as sleep,
Or death, below the troubled deep.
And on the pouting lips of these
Red corals of the silent seas,
Sweet birds, the everlasting seal
Of silence that the God has set
On this dead island, sits for aye.

I would forget, yet not forget
Their helpless eloquence. They creep
Somehow into my heart, and keep
One bleak, cold corner, jewel set.
They steal my better self away
To them, as little birds that day
Stole fruits from out the cherry-trees.

So helpless and so wholly still,
So sad, so wrapt in mute surprise,
That I did love, despite my will.

One little maid of ten, — such eyes,
So large and lonely, so divine, —
Such pouting lips, such peachy cheek, —
Did lift her perfect eyes to mine,
Until our souls did touch and speak;
Stood by me all that perfect day,
Yet not one sweet word could she say.

She turned her melancholy eyes
So constant to my own, that I
Forgot the going clouds, the sky,
Found fellowship, took bread and wine,
And so her little soul and mine
Stood very near together there.
And O, I found her very fair.
Yet not one soft word could she say:
What did she think of all that day?

The sometime song of gondolier
Is heard afar. The fishermen

Betimes draw net by ruined shore,
In full spring time when east winds fall;
Then traders row with muffled oar,
Tedesca or the turban'd Turk,
The pirate, at some midnight work
By watery wall, — but that is all.

XL.

REMOTE, around the lonesome ship,
Old Morgan moved, but knew it not,
For neither star nor moon fell down . . .
I trow that was a lonesome spot
He found, where boat and ship did dip
In sands like some half-sunken town,
And all things rose bat-winged and brown.

At last before the leader lay
A form that in the night did seem
A slain Goliath.
As in a dream,
He drew aside in his slow pace,
And look'd. He saw a sable face,
A friend that fell that very day,
Thrown straight across his wearied way.

He falter'd now. His iron heart,
That never yet refused its part,
Began to fail him ; and his strength
Shook at his knees, as shakes the wind
A shatter'd ship.
His scatter'd mind
Ranged up and down the land. At length
He turn'd, as ships turn, tempest toss'd,
For now he knew that he was lost,
And sought in vain the moon, the stars,
In vain the battle-star of Mars.

Again he moved. And now again
He paused, he peer'd along the plain,
Another form before him lay.
He stood, and statue-white he stood,
He trembled like a stormy wood, —
It was a foeman brown and gray.

He lifted up his head again,

Again he search'd the great profound
For moon, for star, but sought in vain.
He kept his circle round and round;
The great ship lifting from the sand
And pointing heavenward like a hand.

XLI.

AND still he crept along the plain,
Yet where his foeman dead again
Lay in his way he moved around,
And soft as if on sacred ground,
And did not touch him anywhere.
It might have been he had a dread,
In his half-crazed and fever'd brain,
His mortal foe might wake again
If he should dare to touch him there.

He circled round the lonesome ship
Like some wild beast within a wall,
That keeps his paces round and round.
The very stillness had a sound;
He saw strange somethings rise and dip;

He felt the weirdness like a pall
Come down and cover him.

It seem'd
To take a form, take many forms,
To talk to him, to reach out arms;
Yet on he kept, and silent kept,
And as he led he lean'd and slept,
And as he slept he talk'd and dream'd.

Then shadows follow'd, stopp'd, and
stood
Bewildered, wandered back again,
Came on and then fell to the sand
And sinking died.

Then other men
Did wag their woolly heads and laugh,
Then bend their necks and seem to quaff
Of cooling waves that careless flow
Where woods and long strong grasses grow.

Yet on wound Morgan, leaning low,
With head upon his breast, and slow
As hand upon a dial plate.
He did not turn his course or quail,
He did not falter, did not fail,
Turn right or left or hesitate.

Some far-off sounds had lost their way,
And seem'd to call to him and pray
For help, as if they were affright.
It was not day, it seem'd not night,
But that dim land that lies between
The mournful, faithful face of night
And loud and gold-bedazzled day;
A night that was not felt but seen.

There seem'd not then the ghost of sound.
He stepp'd as soft as step the dead;
Yet on he led in solemn tread,
Bewilder'd, blinded, round and round,

About the great black ship that rose
Tall-masted as that ship that blows
Her ghost below lost Panama,—
The tallest mast man ever saw.

Two leaning shadows follow'd him,
Their eyes were red, their teeth shone white,
Their limbs did lift as shadows swim.
Then one went left and one went right,
And in the night pass'd out of night;
Pass'd through the portals black, unknown,
And Morgan totter'd on alone.

XLII.

AND why he still survived the rest,
Why still he had the strength to stir,
Why still he stood like gnarlèd oak
That buffets storm and tempest stroke,
One cannot say, save but for her,
That helpless being on his breast;
At rest; that would not let him rest.

She did not speak, she did not stir;
In rippled currents over her
Her black, abundant hair pour'd down
Like mantle or some sable gown.

That sad, sweet dreamer; she who knew
Not any thing of earth at all,
Nor cared to know its bane or bliss;

That dove that did not touch the land,
That knew, yet did not understand.
And this may be because she drew
Her all of life right from the hand
Of God, and did not choose to learn
The things that make up earth's concern.

Ah! there be souls none understand;
Like clouds, they cannot touch the land,
Drive as they may by field or town.
Then we look wise at this and frown,
And we cry, "Fool," and cry, "Take hold
Of earth, and fashion gods of gold."

. . . Unanchor'd ships, they blow and blow,
Sail to and fro, and then go down
In unknown seas that none shall know,
Without one ripple of renown.
Poor drifting dreamers sailing by,
They seem to only live to die.

Call these not fools; the test of worth
Is not the hold you have of earth.
Lo! there be gentlest souls sea-blown
That know not any harbor known.
Now it may be the reason is
They touch on fairer shores than this.

XLIII.

And dark-eyed Ina? Nestled there,
Half-hidden in her glorious hair,
The while its midnight folds fell down
From out his great arms nude and brown,
She lay against his hairy breast,
All motionless as death, below
His great white beard like shroud, or snow,
As if in everlasting rest.

He totter'd side to side to keep
Erect and keep his steady tread;
He lean'd, he bent to her his head . . .
"She sleeps uncommon sound," he said,
"As if in that eternal sleep,
Where cool and watered willows sweep."

At last he touch'd a fallen group,
Dead fellows tumbled in the sands,
Dead foemen, gather'd to the dead.
And eager now the man did stoop,
Lay down his load and reach his hands,
And stretch his form and look steadfast
And frightful, and as one aghast
And ghostly from his hollow eyes.
He lean'd and then he raised his head,
And look'd for Vasques, but in vain;
He laid his two great arms crosswise,
Took breath a time with trembling main,
Then peered again along the plain.

Lo! from the sands another face,
The last that follow'd through the deep,
Comes on from out the lonesome place.
And Vasques, too, survives!

But where?

His last bold follower lies there,

Thrown straight across old Morgan's track,
As if to check him, bid him back.
He stands, he does not dare to stir,
He watches by his child asleep,
He fears, for her: but only her.
The man who ever mock'd at death,
He hardly dares to draw his breath.

Beyond, and still as black despair,
A man rose up, stood dark and tall,
Stretch'd out his neck, reach'd forth, let fall
Dark oaths, and Death stood waiting there.

He drew his blade, came straight as death
Right up before the follower,
The last of Morgan's sable men,
While Morgan watched aside by her,
And saw his foeman wag his beard
And fiercest visage ever seen.
The while that dead man lay between.

I think no man there drew a breath,
I know that no man quail'd or fear'd.

The tawny dead man stretch'd between,
And Vasques set his foot thereon.
The stars were seal'd, the moon was gone,
The very darkness cast a shade.
The scene was rather heard than seen,
The rattle of a single blade. . . .

A right foot rested on the dead,
A black hand reach'd and clutch'd a beard,
Then neither prayed, nor dreamed of hope . . .
A fierce face reach'd, a fierce face peer'd . . .
No bat went whirling overhead,
No star fell out of Ethiope. . . .

The dead man lay between them there,
The two men glared as tigers glare,
The black man held him by the beard.

He wound his hand, he held him fast,
And tighter held, as if he fear'd
The man might 'scape him at the last.
Whiles Morgan did not speak or stir,
But stood in silent watch by her.

Not long. . . . A light blade lifted, thrust,
A blade that leapt and swept about,
So wizard-like, like wand in spell,
So like a serpent's tongue thrust out . . .
Thrust twice, thrust thrice, thrust as he fell,
Thrust through until it touch'd the dust.

Yet ever as he thrust and smote,
The black hand like an iron band
Did tighten to the gasping throat.
He fell, but did not loose his hand;
The two fell dead upon the sand.

Lo! up and from the fallen forms

Two ghosts came forth like cloud of storms.
Two tall ghosts stood, and looking back,
With hands all bloody, and hands clutch'd,
Strode on together, till they touch'd,
Along the lonesome, chartless track,
Where dim Plutonian darkness fell,
Then touch'd the outer rim of hell,
And looking back their great despair
Sat sadly down as resting there.

XLIV.

PERCHANCE there was a strength in death;
The scene it seem'd to nerve the man
To superhuman strength. He rose,
Held up his head, began to scan
The heavens and to take his breath
Right strong and lustily. He now
Resumed his load, and with his eye
Fixed on a star that filtered through
The farther west, pushed bare his brow,
And kept his course with head held high,
As if he strode his deck and drew
His keel below some lifted light
That watched the rocky reef at night.

How lone he was, how patient she,
Upon that lonesome sandy sea!

It were a sad, unpleasant sight
To follow them through all the night,
Until the time they lifted hand,
And touched at last a watered land.

The turkeys walked the tangled grass,
And scarcely turned to let them pass.
There was no sign of man, or sign
Of savage beast. 'Twas so divine,
It seem'd as if the bended skies
Were rounded for this Paradise.

The large-eyed antelope came down
From off their windy hills, and blew
Their whistles as they wandered through
The open groves of watered wood;
Then came as light as if a-wing,
And reached their noses wet and brown,
And stamped their little feet, and stood
Close up before them wondering.

What if this were the Eden true,
They found in far heart of the new
And unnamed westmost world I sing,
Where date and history had birth,
And man first 'gan his wandering
To go the girdles of the earth!

It lies a little isle mid land,
An island in a sea of sand;
With reedy waters and the balm
Of an eternal summer air.
Some blowy pines toss tall and fair;
And there are grasses long and strong,
And tropic fruits that never fail:
The Manzinetta pulp, the palm,
The prickly pear, with all the song
Of summer birds.
And there the quail
Makes nest, and you may hear her call
All day from out the chaparral.

A land where white man never trod,
And Morgan seems some demi-god,
That haunts the red man's spirit land.
A land where never red man's hand
Is lifted up in strife at all.
He holds it sacred unto those
Who bravely fell before their foes,
And rarely dares its desert wall.

Here breaks nor sound of strife or sign;
Rare times a red man comes this way,
Alone, and battle-scarred and gray,
And then he bends devout before
The maid who keeps the cabin door,
And deems her sacred and divine.

Within the island's heart, 'tis said,
Tall trees are bending down with bread,
And that a fountain pure as truth,
And deep and mossy bound and fair,
Is bubbling from the forest there, —
Perchance the fabled fount of youth!

An isle where never cares betide;
Where solitude comes not, and where
The soul is ever satisfied.
An isle where skies are ever fair,
Where men keep never date nor day,
Where Time has thrown his glass away.

This isle is all their own. No more
The flight by day, the watch by night.
Dark Ina twines about the door
The scarlet blooms, the blossoms white,
And winds red berries in her hair,
And never knows the name of care.

She has a thousand birds; they blow
In rainbow clouds, in clouds of snow;
The birds take berries from her hand;
They come and go at her command.

She has a thousand pretty birds,

That sing her summer songs all day;
Small black-hoofed antelope in herds,
And squirrels bushy-tail'd and gray,
With round and sparkling eyes of pink,
And cunning-faced as you can think.

She has a thousand busy birds;
And is she happy in her isle,
With all her feathered friends and herds?
For when has Morgan seen her smile?

She has a thousand cunning birds,
They would build nestings in her hair;
She has brown antelope in herds;
She never knows the name of care;
Why then is she not happy there?

All patiently she bears her part;
She has a thousand birdlings there,
These birds they would build in her hair;
But not one bird builds in her heart.

She has a thousand birds ; yet she
Would give ten thousand cheerfully,
All bright of plume and loud of tongue,
And sweet as ever trilled or sung,
For one small fluttered bird to come
And sit within her heart, though dumb.

She has a thousand birds ; yet one
Is lost, and, lo ! she is undone.
She sighs sometimes. She looks away,
And yet she does not weep or say.

She has a thousand birds. The skies
Are fashioned for her paradise ;
A very queen of fairy land,
With all earth's fruitage at command,
And yet she does not lift her eyes.
She sits upon the water's brink
As mournful soul'd as you can think.

She has a thousand birds ; and yet
She will look downward, nor forget
The fluttered white-winged turtle dove,
The changeful-throated birdling, love,
That came, that sang through tropic trees,
Then flew for aye across the seas.

The waters kiss her feet ; above
Her head the trees are blossoming,
And fragrant with eternal spring.
Her birds, her antelope are there,
Her birds they would build in her hair ;
She only waits her birdling, love.
She turns, she looks along the plain,
Imploring love to come again.

Cambridge: Press of John Wilson & Son.

MR. MILLER'S

SONGS OF THE SUN-LANDS.

Selections from some criticisms of Mr. Miller's new volume of Poems, which have appeared in the English journals.

From the Athenæum.

"Songs of the Sun-Lands" is, it will be seen, similar in character to "Songs of the Sierras," previously published. The same kind of materials is used, and the same kind of faults and excellence in their use is observable. Mr. Miller's muse in this, its second flight, has taken the same direction as in its first essay, but, upon the whole, we think, with a stronger wing. The new work gives evidence that the author has not, as was feared, intensified his former mannerism, but has profited by the advice of friends and critics.

From the Academy.

Mr. Miller has a faculty of making himself felt through what he writes, and we quit his poems with a mingled sense of admiration and regret: admiration of his really great powers; regret that he seems unable to pursue one of two courses in their application, &c.

From the Westminster Review.

We some time ago called especial attention to this new American poet's first work, "The Songs of the Sierras," nor do we repent of our criticism. He has perhaps lost something of that boldness, and that flavor of originality, which in a certain way reminded one of Walt Whitman without his special weaknesses and extravagances. Still, to counterbalance this loss, he has gained a certain polish. Yet here we perceive a danger. But Mr. Miller must be careful that he does not buy elegance at too dear a price. We ourselves prefer the roughness of the backwoods of America to all the drawing-room conventionalities of Europe. We prefer Mr. Joaquin Miller's native reed-pipe to any guitar. The most perfect poem in the present collection is without doubt "The Isles of the Amazons." Here we see Mr. Miller at his best. Here he has put forth his real strength. It is, in short, a poem which will live.

From the Standard.

No poetry of the present age has any claim to the unconventional freedom, the supreme independence, the spontaneity, the bold and vigorous originality, the all-pervading passion, the unresting energy, and the prodigal wealth of imagery which stamp the poetry before us. . . . For further specimens of Mr. Miller's present poems we must send our readers to the volume itself, which is, with all its faults, a very garden of delight, adorned everywhere as it is with the fairest blooms of fancy, and breathing everywhere as it does of the sweetest and purest inspirations of the muse.

From the London Sunday Times.

The success both in England and America of Mr. Joaquin Miller's "Songs of the Sierras" has been uncontested. The tide of passionate life with which they were charged, and the fervor of poetic appreciation and sympathy they displayed, combined with the startling beauty and power of portions of the workmanship to render men insensible to irregularities and inequalities of style. . . . Here we bid farewell to Mr. Miller's delightful volume. A pleasanter companion into the enchanted gardens of poetry we do not seek. He knows

"each lane and every alley green,
Dingle or bushy dell of the wild wood,
And every bosky bourn from side to side,"

and he conducts us to scenes to which we have no other guide. That Mr. Miller had poetic inspiration his first volume abundantly proved. That his verse will not be a mere well at which the traveller can drink once ere pursuing his journey, but a full river of song hurrying through forest and meadow, and bearing with it carol of bird and scent of flower and hay, is now sufficiently established.

From the Bookseller.

Resembling his previously published collection, in that the verses are principally descriptive of strange, far-away countries, and contain numerous bright, beautiful pictures of external nature, these songs of the sun-lands will be warmly welcomed as the riper efforts of a real poet. . . . And so we might proceed through poem after poem, finding images of great and sterling poetic value. Nor, perhaps, would it be difficult to discover some that might be called trivial and poor; but we prefer to judge a writer by his best rather than by his worst; and Mr. Miller's best lines stamp him a true man, — a man of sympathetic instincts and deep reverence for all that is high and noble in nature and humanity.

From the Nonconformist.

Of all American poetry in recent years, that of Mr. Joaquin Miller is the freshest. He is a new poet in the proper sense of the term. He owes allegiance to no transatlantic masters, and he is no servile imitator of the modern minstrelsy of our own country. In outward form — in the mechanism of his poetry — he of course follows the fashion of the times; but the spirit is new, the tone is individual and distinct. In his poems for the first time the prairies, the sierras, and the new and old life of the Far West of America, have been fairly poetized, so to speak. . . . "Songs of the Sun-Lands" contains nothing, perhaps, superior to "Arizonian" in Mr. Miller's "Songs of the Sierras;" yet it contains no poem so crude as one or two poems in his former volume. The best here is, undoubtedly, "The Isles of the Amazons." . . . Notwithstanding these defects, however, we maintain that we have in Mr. Joaquin Miller a new poet, who with more culture and higher aims is fully capable of producing in the future a poem that the world will not willingly let die.

From the Globe.

His poetry is in no danger of suffering neglect, nor is it likely to lack admirers. By his earlier volume, "The Songs of the Sierras," he fully proved his right to be heard; and students of poetry have not forgotten the influence of the fresh thought and freer music his verse contained. That, in truth, was the essence of Mr. Miller's achievement. He had somehow broken away from the ordinary standards of poetical composition without sacrifice of musical effect. The verse was larger and with less restraint than could be found in other singers, moving with a more continuous flow, and advancing in a cadence always varied and not recurring. Something instructive in the style seemed to image both the singer and the thing sung of, so that we were influenced not so much by this or that particular thought, as by the romantic and picturesque effect of the whole, with its fearless and confident description, and its untamed yet tuneful melody. To follow the poet was like following a keen, swift rider, who rides eagerly, it matters not whither, and who attracts us by a wild grace and a beautiful skill as he rushes through scenes of luxuriant loveliness that would cause a less impetuous horseman to pause and linger. That was the character of his verse as we knew it in the earlier volume, and that also is its character here. What was best in the earlier work is retained in this, and it still remains the best the poet can do.

From the Morning Post.

The author appears to be a true poet, with all the natural fire and tenderness — the spark and dew — that fall from Helicon. . . . In the present collection of poems he has largely contributed to his own fame, which was already very great, and to the pleasure of all who can listen with sympathy to the pathetic muse expressing her feelings in simple but inspired strains.

SONGS OF THE SIERRAS.

BY JOAQUIN MILLER.

Extracts from some Reviews of the New American Poet, which have appeared in the English Literary Journals—the Criticisms of some of the most learned Critics of the day.

"ENGLISH criticism is discerning and deliberate. Books by new authors are sometimes put aside because their authors are unknown: but if a work is read at all, it will be, except in very rare instances, candidly and fairly criticised, and public opinion will tolerate neither undue severity nor undue praise. English criticism (except perhaps that of a few of the lowest journals, which is not worth having) is not to be bought with favors or with gold. Faults are not absent from it; but venality or absolute unfairness is not of these. If ever they become so, the public will quench the critics.

"Miller came to London friendless, without influence, without reputation. His book won for itself the admiration of some of the best and wisest of the land. Many of the most favorable notices which have appeared in the chief Journals and Reviews, have been written by the most trained and cautious hands in London. The men who have clustered about him have won the highest fame the country can bestow through years of honorable and splendid toil. Their opinion stands as the index of the world's opinion. Higher favors the world has not to bestow than their friendship and esteem."

GEORGE FRANCIS ARMSTRONG.

SONGS OF THE SIERRAS.

THE ENGLISH PRESS.

The Spectator.

It has for some time been a matter of speculation to Englishmen whether the new life of the English race in the Far West would produce a new growth of poetry. Bret Harte and the author of these *Songs of the Sierras* have now removed the question from the region of speculation to the region of fact. There are, indeed, other American poets of older standing, whose claims we are far from depreciating; Mr. Lowell, for instance, is, in our judgment, entitled to stand in the very first rank of living writers of English. But he and his colleagues of the Eastern States must be regarded by us, and we trust they do not refuse to regard themselves, as continuing and developing the already mature literature of the mother country rather than as the founders of a new culture. The poetry of Lowell or Wendell Holmes is distinguished, indeed, from that of their English contemporaries by a character and local color and humor which are national as well as individual; yet we feel that its groundwork is, in substance, the same. The same complex and advanced civilization rules men's thoughts in Boston and in London. It is far otherwise in the remoter districts, where there exists not a transplanted, fairly homogeneous society, but a society which has formed, or is still forming, itself on the spot from the concourse of all kinds of elements; and we might well be anxious that the comparatively primitive life of the West should find a poetical exponent before its first freshness is crystallized into the forms of older communities. Certain English critics are disposed to accept Walt Whitman as such; but whatever may be his individual merits — and our own estimate of them would be very different from what his admirers claim for him — he is so isolated and erratic that he cannot be taken as representing anything beyond the promptings of his own fancy; whether his peculiarities are due to excess of eccentricity or to want of education, they, at all events, make him too singular to be a type. Now Mr. Miller's work has a real significance beyond what appears on the face of it. It brings the first-fruits, and the promise of a new soil. It shows a true revival of primitive life in its vigor, simplicity, and occasional rudeness. Its merits and defects are those of confident and over-lusty youth, and the defects, with one exception, which will presently be mentioned, are venial.

It is not pretended that Mr. Miller's poetry, or even his language, is faultless. There are obvious inequalities, blemishes, and slips of language; much work roughly, some incorrectly done; but in spite of all drawbacks, the fact remains that when one has taken up the volume it is very difficult to put it down; and such a fact in the case of a writer who has ample time before him to perfect his style outweighs a multitude of shortcomings in detail. The nature of these minor defects will sufficiently appear in the course of the extracts to be given, and for the reason just mentioned they do not affect our general estimate; it is therefore needless to dwell on them. The constant use of the periphrastic conjugation wlth the auxiliary verb *do* in places where the principal verb does not require any emphasis, is the only fault of style that has struck us distinctly and obtrusively.

That which is first to fix the attention as a prominent quality in Mr. Miller's poems is the faculty of transmitting direct and vivid impressions of outward nature. In the older countries, the value of an artist's observations is in danger of decreasing at the same time that the perfection of the instruments for recording them is being increased. It is difficult for any one within the immediate influence of a European culture, if he does not possess original power of a very rare quality, not to mix up his actual experience with preconceived ideas of what his experience ought to be; and therefore in the world of art, not less than in any other world, great is the multitude of those who seek their life and lose it. On the other hand, the best part of Mr. Miller's work belongs to a stage of thought at which seeking has hardly begun; he can lose his life in nature, and has the reward of finding it. This description of a storm breaking, which occurs very early in the volume, is enough to show the presence of no common power:—

"I lay in my hammock: the air was heavy
And hot, and threatening; the very heaven
Was holding its breath; and bees in a bevy
Hid under my thatch; and birds were driven
In clouds to the rocks in a hurried whirr
As I peer'd down by the path for her;
She stood like a bronze bent over the river,
The proud eyes fix'd, the passion unspoken,
When the heavens broke like a great dyke broken.
Then, ere I fairly had time to give her
A shout of warning, a rushing of wind
And the rolling of clouds and a deafening din,
And a darkness that had been black to the blind
Came down, as I shouted, 'Come in! come in!
Come under the roof, come up from the river,
As up from a grave,—come now, or come never!'
The tassell'd tops of the pines were as weeds,
The red-woods rock'd like to lake-side reeds,
And the world seem'd darken'd and drown'd forever."

The horror of sudden darkness could not be more forcibly brought out than in the line we have italicized, and, so far as we know, the expression is quite new; at any rate, the whole scene was fresh in the writer's mind. If it be asked who she was that bent over the river, the answer is not altogether satisfactory. She is the same person who appears throughout the book in slightly varying apparel; a Byronic lay-figure transported to the mountains and prairies, and looking amongst them even more tawdry and artificial than at home. This is the one serious fault which is apparent in Mr. Joaquin Miller's poems. An excessive admiration for Byron has led him into a following of Byron's least admirable manner, by which he often does himself grave injustice. Instead of being strong and natural, as he can be when he is content to be himself, he every now and then tries to be a shadow of Byron, and so becomes artificial and turgid. The poem entitled "Californian" is all but spoilt by this unfortunate propensity. And the same cause makes it quite impossible to say at present what may be his real power of insight into character. There are some signs indeed that Mr. Miller has observed men; but until the Byronic glamour is removed from his eyes, he has no chance of really seeing a woman. Time and wider experience may be trusted, we hope, to give him courage to look at humanity, as he has looked at the forests and the sierras, with the untrammelled strength of his own eyes. As it is, Mr. Miller is often happy in dealing with single phases of emotion. There is true and spontaneous poetry in this painting (from *With Walker in Nicaragua)*:—

"O passion-tossed and bleeding past,
Part now, part well, part wide apart,
As ever ships on ocean slid
Down, down the sea, hull, sail, and mast;
And in the album of my heart
Let hide the pictures of your face,
With other pictures in their place,
Slid over like a coffin's lid."

But to return to the power of sympathy with nature, by which the new poet most chiefly makes good his claim; the same freshness of vision, which gives such force and truth to his direct descriptions, works in his mind a revival of the old myth-forming energy. His soul goes forth to the sun, or the ocean, or the mountain snows, as did the soul of ancient men in days long past. In short, he makes myths over again, quite unaffected by their having been made and fixed in mythology once or many times before. Thus he looks at the mountains after sunset:—

"When the red-curtain'd west has bent red as with weeping,
Low over the couch where the prone day lay dying,
I have stood with brow lifted, confronting the mountains
That held their white faces of snow in the heavens,
And said, 'It is theirs to array them so purely,
Because of their nearness to the temple eternal;'
And childlike have said, 'They are fair resting-places
For the dear, weary dead on their way up to heaven.'"

The peculiar unrhymed metre of this extract will be noticed. Mr. Miller employs it in long passages, and with considerable effect. We find, again, a very old piece of sun-mythology revived in all the vigor of youth, and joyfully ignoring the fate of its eastern kindred, how they have died and been embalmed, and are now in process of dissection by comparative philology:—

"Where mountains repose in their blueness,
Where the sun first lands in his newness,
And marshals his beams and his lances,
Ere down to the vale he advances
With visor raised, and rides swiftly
On the terrible night in his way,
And slays him, and with his sword deftly
Hews from him the beautiful day,
Lay nestled the town of Renalda."

We must go a long way back to parallel this thorough and unartificial transfusion of nature with human life. The sea, too, is alive as the moderns can seldom make him:—

"The warm sea fondled with the shore,
And laid his white face on the sands."

* * * * * *

We give one more example from Mr. Miller, the more interesting in that myth, metaphor, and description are to be seen all blending into one another. A mountaineer is speaking with a stranger, who is wandering in disgust with the world:—

"At night, o'erspread by the rich purple robe,
The deep, imperial, Tyrian hue that folds
The invisible form of the eternal God,
You will see the sentry stars come marching forth
And take their posts upon the field above,
Around the great white tent where sleeps their chief;
You will hear the kakea singing in a dream
The wildest, sweetest song a soul can drink;
And when the tent is folded up, and all
The golden-fringed sentries faced about
To let the pompous day-king pass along,
We two will stand upon a sloping hill,
Where white-lipped springs come leaping, laughing up,
With water spouting forth in merry song,
Like bridled mirth from out a school-girl's throat,
And look far down the bending Willamette,
And in his thousand graceful curves and strokes,
And strange meanderings, men misunderstand,
Read the unutterable name of God.

DON CARLOS.

"Why, truly now, this fierce and broken land,
Seen through your eyes, assumes a fairer shape.
Lead up, for you are nearer God than I."

The poem called "Ina," from which this is taken, is in form dramatic. It hardly pretends to any unity of construction, but there is often great merit in the dialogue, and Mr. Miller has grappled with the difficulties of dramatic blank verse far more successfully than most of those who attempt the metre which is apparently the easiest, and really the most difficult, that a writer of English verse can choose. Indeed Mr. Miller's is almost always melodious, though in some places attention is required to seize the rhythm. Once or twice there is a startling resemblance to Mr. Swinburne's metrical effects, as in these stanzas of Ina's song:—

"O hearts fill'd of fevers, of fires,
Reaching forth from the tangible blossoms,
Reaching far for impossible things;
Beat not nor break your warm wings
On the cruel, cold bars any more.

* * * * * *

Leaves fade, and the frosts are before us;
Leaves fall, and the winter winds are;
Loves fail! Let us cross and deplore us;
Loves die! Lift your hands as at war;
Lift your hands to the world and deny it;
Lift your voice, cry aloud, and deny;
Cry aloud ''Tis a lie!' and belie it,
With lives made a beautiful lie."

However, we do not believe the resemblance was intended. Rather the coincidence shows that Mr. Swinburne's manner is not so artificial or unnatural as is commonly supposed.

There is yet to be noticed another piece of evidence, valuable because quite undesigned, of the primitive atmosphere of thought in which these poems were written. Thrice the speaker is represented counting on his fingers, not as civilized man may do, using them only as an aid or check, but as the savage does, to whom they are the sole instrument and symbol of numeration:—

"I lifted my fingers
And fell to counting the round years over,
That I had dwelt where the sun goes down.
Four full hands, and a finger over!"

"They were so few,
I near could count them on one hand."

"I count my fingers over, so,
And find it years and years ago."

The significance of this will readily be seen by readers who have Mr. Tylor's chapter on finger-counting fresh in their memories. It has been made to appear, we trust, that the virtues of Mr. Miller's poetry are of a kind likely to be further developed, and the faults of a kind likely to be outgrown. If he escapes the dangers of premature success (and he has the strength to escape them), he may well achieve far greater things in the future.

The Athenæum.

THERE is a current notion that American poetry should be different in kind from ours—should, in the slang of criticism, "be racy of the soil from which it springs." Rivers of prodigious length, vast prairies and forests, and huge mountain-ranges, must, it is believed, reflect themselves in the productions of the native poet. We hesitate to share this belief. The bold pioneers who first penetrate the wilderness are too deeply engrossed in material concerns to occupy themselves with the divine art; and, when the wilderness becomes the seat of a dense population, its inhabitants live under conditions such as we.

As far, at least, as literature is concerned, the Americans are not, as Mr. Lowell contends, of yesterday. The man of the New World, inheriting our language, inherits also our history, traditions, religion, modes of thought; and these no physical peculiarities of cou... y are influential enough to countervail. He is heir to Shakespeare equally with the man of Middlesex or of Warwick. Of this the volume under notice is corroboration. Mr. Miller has spent his whole life in the wild woods and mountains of Western America, and yet is not an American of the type anticipated. "Polished bronzes," "chiselled marble," "Italian skies," "Grecian forms," have meaning to him; and he has had dreams of dead and living poets the memory of which remains.

First in place, and, we may add, in excellence, is "Arizonian," so named from that western territory within which the scene is laid.

* * * * * *

There is much beauty in the idea which forms the basis of the poem; but the treatment is frequently crude and unsatisfactory. Mr. Miller has himself described his work as rough quartz; and he is not inaccurate. We find the gold to be of finest quality; but the proportion it bears to the baser material is small. As will be seen from the quotations we have made, the poems show traces of the influence of our best modern poets. Mr. Miller, however, is no copyist. If he has made other men his models, his life, experience, and nature have the effect of giving to his production a freshness and an originality obviously due to his own individuality. He resembles Mr. Browning in novel and apt metaphors taken from objects high or low, common or uncommon, but always new and forcible, and often quaint—making one smile at the sudden turn. So also he is like Mr. Browning in his homely strokes of humor.

* * * * * *

Mr. Miller is best in his lyrical compositions. He has a keen, and close, and attentive perception of nature, personal and external, and he is a clear, and accurate, and picturesque painter of its moods. His blank and unrhymed verse is bad: it is spasmodic and bombastic.

* * * * * *

In the lyrical poems we light upon incidents represented with great beauty and dramatic force; but here, when we most expect evidence of dramatic power, we are disappointed. The author is clearly unable to develop a character dramatically. His descriptions are all objective. Even subjective feelings are made objective, and treated objectively.

The other poems in the volume are inferior to "Arizonian." "With Walker in Nicaragua" is occasionally tame, but there are parts of it extremely grand. The end of "Californian," a long poem relating to life in the gold regions, is as fine as anything in the book, but the piece itself is not well sustained. "The Last Taschastas" is a graphic poem, in which the author revels in descriptions of chiefs, and the brown and red beauties of the Indian tribes, and shows his deep sympathy with those who are driven back by the white man and civilization. Although we cannot give Mr. Miller a front place in the hierarchy of modern poets, we are glad to welcome him as a true and original singer. "Songs of the Sierras" is a volume which must be read by all lovers of real poetry.

The Saturday Review.

WHATEVER the faults of style which disfigure Mr. Miller's poems—and they are many and flagrant—there can be no doubt that he possesses the genuine poetic faculty. He writes because he cannot help it—the best reason of all—perhaps the only justifiable reason for composing poetry. The snowy Sierra and the tropical cañon, the roving, adventurous borderer's life, the stirring tales of hunt and foray, all these supplied materials pregnant with romance and poetry, and only required to be transmuted into words. This task Mr. Miller has attempted, and the fact that his lines glow with tropical passion, and that his descriptions transport us in imagination to the scenes among which they were composed, compels us to forgive him for the lawlessness with which he tramples on the conventional limitations of art.

The poems are but seven in number, and amongst them the first two are, to our mind, considerably the best. The first is entitled "Arizonian."

* * * * * *

www.ingramcontent.com/pod-product-compliance
Lightning Source LLC
LaVergne TN
LVHW011208110826
845150LV00006B/1367

9781425517885